D0440371

The Unheard Voices

DISCARD

DISCARD

The Unheard Voices

Community Organizations and Service Learning

Edited by

Randy Stoecker and
Elizabeth A. Tryon
With Amy Hilgendorf

Temple University Press
Philadelphia

Temple University Press
1601 North Broad Street
Philadelphia PA 19122
www.temple.edu/tempress

Copyright © 2009 by Temple University

All rights reserved

Published 2009

The material used in Chapter 4 has also appeared in "The Challenge of
Short-Term Service Learning," *Michigan Journal of Community Service
Learning* 14, no. 2 (Spring 2008) and is used with permission.

Some findings in this book are summarized in "The Unheard Voices:
Community Organizations and Service Learning," *Journal of Higher
Education Outreach and Engagement* 12, no. 3 (Fall 2008).

♾ The paper used in this publication meets the requirements of
the American National Standard for Information Sciences—Permanence
of Paper for Printed Library Materials, ANSI Z39.48-1992

Library of Congress Cataloging-in-Publication Data

The unheard voices : community organizations and service learning /
edited by Randy Stoecker and Elizabeth A. Tryon with Amy Hilgendorf.
    p. cm.
  Includes bibliographical references and index.
    ISBN 978-1-59213-994-1 (cloth : alk. paper)—ISBN 978-1-59213-995-8
(pbk. : alk. paper)
    1. Community organization.   2. Service learning.   3. Social action.
  I. Stoecker, Randy, 1959–   II. Tryon, Elizabeth A.
    HM766.U64 2009
    378.1'03—dc22   2008047854

Printed in the United States of America

2 4 6 8 9 7 5 3

Contents

Preface

RANDY STOECKER AND ELIZABETH TRYON

Introduction

Our goal in this book is to amplify the unheard voices of community organization staff in the service learning relationship. Except in the individual relationships that they have with students and a small number of truly committed faculty, these voices have not been heard—and they have a lot to say.

Admittedly, however, any attempt by those of us on the academic side of the service learning relationship to present the voices of the community organization staff will necessarily be colored by our own filters, so we want you to know something about the editors and the contributors to this collection, along with the process of its production. We sometimes speak collectively and sometimes individually in this preface.

This Project

This has been a unique project from the beginning. When Randy Stoecker arrived at the University of Wisconsin in Madison, he was almost immediately swept up in the energy surrounding what is known as "The Wisconsin Idea." Everyone, it seemed, was trying to bring the resources of the university to issues in the state's communities. It quickly became clear, however, that the methods for trying to do good through academia had not fully jelled. Most of the outreach work of the university's faculty and students was being done from the perspective of the academy—using its language and forms of understanding—and Randy began hearing from community organization staff about the shortcomings of that model. Elizabeth Tryon (Beth to those who know her well) came to the project as a graduate student through Edgewood College, but also as a staff member at the college's interdisciplinary program that involves community engagement. Her immersion in the small faith-based college model of service learning was producing the same questions.

This book, then, is the result of the community-based research propelled by those concerns. We discuss how the research project originated (with the community organizations), how the process was designed (in collaboration with community organization staff), and how the research has led to several other follow-up action steps (planned and led by community organization staff). One part of the community feedback led to another action research project that involved focus group sessions to assess what types of access to higher education nonprofits would prefer and what vehicle they would like to use for that access. Still in an exploratory phase is a process to determine the feasibility of a nonprofit resource center to possibly broker some of that access.

The starting point for this book was the findings produced by student teams in a community-based qualitative research seminar, based on interviews with sixty-seven community organization staff. Small teams of students took responsibility for drafting chapters of each theme in the findings. This collection, then, is unusual first because it is not a hodgepodge of separate articles about separate data sets or cases, but linked chapters written from the same data. The chapter authors, with the exception of Randy, were all undergraduate or graduate students at the time the chapters were written.

The two of us, then, are editors in a much more intrusive sense than is normally the case in a collection of articles. The initial seminar chapter assignment did not include any introductory material, literature review, citations, or attention to style consistency. As a result, we devoted much more effort to framing each chapter with the relevant literature, editing for style, and adding new material where the theory needed more documentation or analysis. In doing so, however, we did everything possible to preserve the core of the students' work. We may have moved a section here or there, and added or deleted an occasional quote, but we did not change any interpretations or analysis. Amy Hilgendorf then went through each chapter with us, questioning wording and correcting some of the confusion we would sometimes inadvertently introduce in our attempts for clarity.

We believed that the students should remain the primary authors of the chapters. We only added ourselves as authors where we substantially changed the structure and framing of a chapter, with the exception of Chapter 6, on which Beth was an original student author. And we did almost no editing of the chapter written by Amy Mondlach, wanting the reader to hear at least one unfiltered community organization staff voice.

The progression of the process really didn't have any precedent that we knew of, so we have tried to fit our editing roles into the commonly used publishing terminology for lack of better terms. Perhaps out of sheer naïveté, the project was a grand high-wire experiment without a net, because we didn't know we should have one! When we started the seminar, we weren't thinking, "Oh, by the way, let's do this research in a way that we've never seen tried before, and then let's turn it into a book!" Rather, as the findings seemed rather provocative to us, we coeditors were interested in the results as they related to our daily work, and so we decided to go back into the raw material and flesh it out.

The Editors

Randy: I have been trying to be a useful academic ever since I was brought up short by a community activist more than twenty years ago, when I was just a graduate student. He accused me of being just another exploitive academic, extracting the community's information to use for my own career advancement rather than for the good of the community. He, and another community activist who took me under his wing when I was a young assistant professor, taught me how to be useful. It was painful learning, and it gave me an impatiently critical distaste for most of what passes as community engagement in academia.

Consequently, I have developed admittedly deep concerns about service learning, including the variant of service learning that uses community-based research. My own research is showing that there is too little empowerment or capacity building coming from our efforts.

Part of my worry has developed from what I have learned from the leaders in service learning. I remember going to weekend seminars where we attended lectures for eight hours a day about how to conduct service learning, with no attempt to either model or even discuss the facilitation skills necessary to do it in an empowering way. At a particular seminar, which gathered people from around the country on a university campus for three days, I confronted one of those symbolic experiences that stays in your memory forever and begs to be written about. We had just finished an afternoon of stupefying lectures, and a group of us were walking to dinner at the nearest campus dining hall, led by one of the country's most famous service learning proponents. A group ahead of us was veering off the normal route—it was about a half block longer, but traversed a bucolic part of campus rather than the noisy street. I had taken the route myself earlier and was thinking we would just veer off like the other group, when suddenly our famous service learning leader asked in his most professorial voice, "Where are they going?" Since no one else said anything, I explained that they were taking a more scenic route. His disgust was unmistakable: "But this way is shorter. They don't know what they're doing!"

In an early article we sent out about one part of this research, two of the three reviewers were in absolute denial that community organization staff could possibly be dissatisfied with the way institutions practice service learning. One of them, perhaps the same service learning proponent who couldn't understand there is more than one path to dinner, referred to our interviewees as "a disgruntled minority" of community organization staff.

This is the attitude that is limiting service learning. The dominant service learning proponents have decided what is best for the community, or have never gotten past the exploitive mind-set of using the community as a way to educate their students. This is of course not everyone, and hopefully not even most of us. We are even beginning to witness that change is in the wind as we hear from other service learning practitioners who are trying to change their own practice to integrate and serve community development goals. For me, then, this project is part of a growing effort to develop service learning not by pronouncing truths but by proposing processes, and not by lecturing but by listening. I must admit that my own approach to service learning has been significantly altered by this project. I was one of those professors who sent my students out without talking with the community organization staff first, requiring only fifteen to twenty hours of service, and with no clear learning or project plan. I was the community organization director's service learning nightmare. I am, as a result of this research, trying to move toward becoming useful, with the guidance of my community partners who are now becoming my friends.

Beth: I came to this project with a special interest in the views of community organizations, derived from fifteen years' experience running a nonprofit in music education, coupled with my last four years as a community partner specialist at a small private college. One of the components I help facilitate in an academic program called "Human Issues Studies" is to seek and arrange service learning with faculty, students, and community organizations. This peripatetic background has given me a dualistic perspective on these issues.

Before I had ever heard the term "service learning," I codirected and performed in a grassroots-level arts organization with my husband. We were touring and recording artists for decades, but wanted to work more during the school day to be home with our kids at night. We devised an original method for teaching jazz improvisation and composition at public elementary and middle schools in low-income communities. We also worked everywhere else we could get hired— in libraries, museums, community and neighborhood centers, Boys & Girls Clubs, Big Brothers Big Sisters events, and children's festivals throughout the Midwest, Florida, and even Puerto Rico.

Once, we almost inadvertently created a riot during our first outreach concert at a summer camp for disadvantaged youth. As we usually did in the public schools, we gave a short introduction of the types of instruments, a brief theory lesson, and then asked for volunteers to take one of our pieces of musical equipment and join an improvised composition that we would spontaneously conceive together. The problem was that we had not been briefed on numbers or the structure of the day camp. We had about thirty instruments, and there were more than eighty kids. Even though we had explained that everyone would get a turn during the hour, they were more conditioned to having to scrap with each other for treats, play equipment, and other items of scarcity. Unlike in the schools, there was minimal supervision and poor guidance by staff.

As a result, the children *all* pounced at once! Kids were pulling shakers from each other, grabbing keyboards, knocking each other down, hitting each other over the head with the rhythm sticks, and shouting. The lady from the arts funder who had just arrived to evaluate the program swooped in and seized our microphone, proceeding to harangue the kids—that we artists had come "all the way down here" to "help" them, and how dare they act like "animals." I wanted the floor to open up and swallow me. How could we not have understood that this would be a different situation than in the schools? Order was finally restored, but at the expense of our dignity and the kids' too. Had I been a typical nineteen-year-old college girl from small-town Wisconsin, I'd have had negative stereotypes reinforced, been thoroughly chagrined, and probably never would have attempted to work with minorities again.

Now, having worked for the past four years doing this community outreach work from within academia, I draw from those kinds of experiences, and thus feel a sense of urgency to help improve the interactions between college and community to ensure that students not only have good learning experiences but also that they do no harm. I want to help increase capacity for the community organizations and at the same time make it possible for more students to become more engaged citizens. I am fortunate to be able to collaborate with many dedicated and conscientious faculty members who are making every effort to practice the best possible service learning they can, and I hope the words of the community contained in this volume can help give them the tools they need. Each time I go out to make a presentation at academic conferences and symposia on this research, I see more nods of agreement and hear more stories of other practitioners wanting to move beyond the limitations of our current service learning models.

Thank-Yous

There are many people to thank for the actual book development. First and foremost among those who laid the groundwork for this book is Dr. Margaret Nellis. Margaret's history of trying to bring the university into the community on the community's terms is unsurpassed in Madison. It was Margaret who first drove Randy around Madison to hear how community organization staff were reacting to university outreach efforts. Margaret helped organize the early stages of the research project and assisted with the seminar that produced the original chapters.

We are, of course, deeply grateful to the student authors and the community organization director who contributed the chapter drafts. The students pored through sixty-seven transcripts for hours and hours to produce the findings contained in these pages. We particularly want to recognize Jason Gonzalez and Shannon Bell, who continued on with the project to add resources to the Web site and recruit organization staff to planning meetings as we transitioned into the implementation phase of the project. Katherine Bolton was not part of the original seminar, but joined it later as a Service Learning Fellow through the University of Wisconsin Morgridge Center for Public Service, and was also an instrumental part of the implementation process. Amy Hilgendorf, who joined the seminar as an AmeriCorps°VISTA volunteer, continued to support the project through a position with the University of Wisconsin Cooperative Extension, and then came back to help edit the chapters as a graduate student, has also been invaluable to this project.

We must also thank the community organization staff people who so generously gave their time to create the data, review the students' work, and stay involved through our attempts to make service learning work better. The administrators responsible for community engagement and service learning at the University of Wisconsin, Edgewood College, and Madison Area Technical College also graciously supported this research. The University of Wisconsin Morgridge Center for Public Service provided a small grant to support this project and Edgewood College provided release time for Beth Tryon to continue this project.

Of course, this would not be a book if Temple University Press senior acquisitions editor Mick Gusinde-Duffy hadn't hobbled out from a conference booth on an injured ankle in 2007 to meet with Randy about this work. Mick found us a couple of wonderfully supportive and keenly observant reviewers, and has moved amazingly quickly to put this work into production. Temple published Randy's very first book, and it is nice to return home again. In particular, we would like to thank Gary Kramer, Charles Ault, Emily Taber, and Meredith Phillips, of the Press, and the copyeditors of the Westchester Book editorial staff who provided such a wonderfully supportive editing job.

We also have our individual thank-yous to those who have supported and sustained us throughout this process. The collaborative process of shaping the material of this volume into a coherent whole took many, many hours. First were the hours we spent working through the chapters face-to-face, but more important were the nights and weekends; though spent at home, they nonetheless involved secluding ourselves behind a computer screen working intensely at the editing.

Randy: Tammy Raduege, my spouse of twenty years and partner of twenty-seven years, and Haley Stoecker, my daughter of sixteen years, have become somewhat accustomed to my odd academic schedule that sucks up too many nights and weekends and sends me on too many trips to distant lands. They gave up even more of my time and attention for this book, and not always without forcing me to reflect on my own priorities, for which I am deeply grateful. Academic work can be all-consuming—the concept of the absentminded professor isn't embedded in our culture for nothing. Tammy, thankfully, has an unerring sense of balance, and a strength of voice and depth of love to let me know when my academic obsessions upset that balance. I would also like to thank Lady the standard poodle for her uncounted hours of consistent companionship through the writing process. I imagine there are other writers who understand the role of a loyal dog in the writing process; she is not exactly my muse, but she is definitely my muse's best friend. Finally, I want to acknowledge my coeditor, Beth. It is exceedingly rare to find a student interested in exactly the issues you are working on, even more rare to find one with the dedication to put so many hours into a book project without any guaranteed rewards, and almost impossible to find one willing to be a collaborator rather than just a student.

Beth: My husband, Ted Petith, and fourteen-year-old son, Miles Tryon-Petith, had no clue what they were in for when I brazenly accepted this writing challenge. They nonetheless provided loving support and patience while I ignored trivialities like dinner to "bang away on the computer" after work and into the wee hours of the night, while our trusty beagle-mix, Hershey, lay faithfully at my feet, patiently waiting until I finished a section before walking him. My grown children, Charmaine Swan and Clayton Tryon-Petith, listened kindly to my ruminations and contributed their perspectives as recent college students. I must also thank coeditor Randy Stoecker for his incredible generosity in sharing credits, encouraging me to lead presentations, and helping shape the type of community-focused professional I aspire to be; my supervisor, Dean Pribbenow, for encouraging this work and allowing release time to pursue my graduate classes, interviews, meetings, and presentations; and Kris Mickelson and other faculty colleagues at Edgewood College who have given me much advice and encouragement, especially Denis Collins, an accomplished service learning practitioner who read some early drafts and shared historical references and social justice philosophies.

Onward

This project has taught us that we have much work to do to transform service learning into a practice that serves communities. This book is an initial step along that path. We have talked to the frontline staff in nonprofit organizations. We have not yet taken on the much bigger project of talking to the members of the communities that encounter those service learners.

Our universities and colleges are indeed reaching out, but are not yet fully inviting people in. The challenges created by such an uneven partnership model are particularly evident in service learning. But the willingness of the service learning offices at the University of Wisconsin, Edgewood College, and the Madison Area Technical College to support our efforts to make service learning more community driven is heartening. Since this project began, we have seen community groups become more vocal about their needs, faculty become better listeners, and service learning offices become much more willing to invite the community in rather than simply reach out. We offer this critique of service learning, then, in the same spirit that our community organization representatives gave it. None of them said they were going to give up on service learning. Neither are we.

▌ Unheard Voices

*Community Organizations
and Service Learning*

RANDY STOECKER AND ELIZABETH TRYON

Who Is Served by Service Learning?

E very year, tens of thousands of college students make their way into the community in the name of service learning. They tutor, paint, serve soup, build databases, conduct surveys, organize meetings, run errands, and all manner of other things. Many of them, maybe even the majority, do it to meet a college or university graduation requirement, to receive course credit, or both.

Service learning has now become an institutionalized practice in higher education. From small community colleges to the most prestigious PhD-granting institutions, the practice of sending students into communities that are defined as disadvantaged has become a part of the curriculum and even the requirements of an increasing number of higher education institutions. A lot of institutional hype accompanies these students, and much research promotes the positive impact the practice has on student grades, attitudes, and sensitivities (Lansverk, 2004; Ender et al., 2000; Mooney and Edwards, 2001; Myers-Lipton, 1998; Parker-Gwin and Mabry, 1998; Krain and Nurse, 2004).

There are also claims of the positive impact that service learning has on communities but, as we find, there is much less research to back up those claims (Cruz and Giles, 2000). Consequently, making service learning work for communities may be easier said than done. Finding the right fit between student, agency, and institution is like a huge 3-D jigsaw puzzle. When it works, luck is as important as planning. Elizabeth Tryon (Beth) is a community partner specialist at Edgewood College:

> Recently, an old friend who is head of a community agency called to ask if I knew of any students that would be able to help carry out a grant-funded neighborhood survey for a community project, with a lot of flexibility in scheduling and a small stipend. It was important to him that I focus on recruiting students of color, as the survey would take place in a diverse neighborhood and he felt that respondents would be more comfortable talking to someone that reflected their diversity. And he said, of course it would be too much to ask, but if they spoke even a bit of Spanish, that would be invaluable in some of the neighborhoods. I couldn't think of anyone off the top of my head that was looking for an internship but said I'd post the opportunity on the board.
>
> I hung up the phone and ten minutes later a student-friend walked into the office and said, "I need a job! But only part-time, and the hours have to be flexible!" And . . . he's a bilingual Latino. Hello—this was my lucky day. I gave him the phone number of the agency and he called immediately to take the job. When I got home from work there was a message from my agency friend, basically amazed that I had found someone that fit his dream list so fast.
>
> Usually it's much harder to make that perfect match. I'm on the board of a fledgling nonprofit that heavily relies on field students each semester, particularly with their Youth Court, which keeps young offenders out of the system for first minor offenses by trying them by a jury of their peers. I had put out a call in the Social Science Department, but not heard back from anyone. The executive director was scrambling for assistance, as the program was taking off—what to do? I can't force students to take specific internships; the work has to fit their needs, too.

I followed up again with a faculty member I'd already bugged twice. She said she'd like to help, but assumed this organization didn't have an MSW-qualified supervisor for her students, which was a requirement in her field. I called the board president and found out she is degreed and licensed in social work. When I e-mailed the faculty member, she said, "Good to know—I'll keep that in mind for the future; all my practicum are already placed this semester." The next day she called and said, "Guess what? A new transfer student just walked in and wants an internship now! And she's interested in legal work, particularly juveniles."

Those lucky connections are rare and sometimes take months to find. It's also a time-intensive process, which is certainly a problem for faculty when there is no community partner liaison to help them make matches.

Consequently, there has been growing dissatisfaction among many people both inside and outside the service learning movement since the 1990s, particularly when it comes to the issue of whether service learning truly serves communities. In the worst cases, analysts saw poor communities exploited as free sources of student education (Eby, 1998). Others worried that the "charity" model of service learning reinforced negative stereotypes and students' perceptions of poor communities as helpless (Morton, 1995; Kahne and Westheimer, 1996; Brown, 2001; Marullo and Edwards, 2000; Ward and Wolf-Wendel, 2000). And then there was the concern that the connection between what was happening in the classroom and what was happening in the community was tenuous at best (Eyler and Giles, 1999).

These perceived problems with service learning might be traced to its explosion in the 1980s, influenced by higher education faculty and administrators who were distressed by the increasingly self-centered conservatism of their students (Hutchison, 2001). They believed that finding ways to confront students with actual poor people would help reverse the trend, and service learning began to focus on changing students rather than changing communities. There is nothing wrong with wanting to illuminate college students about the real world before they graduate and venture out into it unprepared, never forced to confront the externalities of the status quo and thus becoming part of the problem. It is also valid to be perturbed with the disconnect between young people privileged enough to attend college and the people of the disinvested communities in which they volunteer. We agree with the view that, because of the status and resources allocated to higher education, those who receive and provide higher education have an obligation to redress the consequences of such inequality.

What we disagree with is the lack of attention given to the question of whether service learning is in fact impacting inequality at the community level in ways that empower community members and build capacity in community organizations. Despite this seemingly common-sensical notion of evaluating the community impact of service learning, the bias in focus toward student outcomes has continued to this day, producing a voluminous literature (Ward and Wolf-Wendel, 2000). Indeed, some writers promote service learning for students with little to no consideration of its impact on communities (Reed et al., 2005; Fitch, 2005; Metz and Youniss, 2003; Honnet and Poulson, 1989). In contrast, while lip service is paid to the importance of community outcomes (Jones, 2003; Kellogg Commission, 1999; Campus Compact, 2003), there are only a handful of studies that look at community impact and community perceptions of service learning (Cruz and Giles, 2000), and these studies have seldom asked the community to help define what community impact should be. While Cruz and Giles (2000) attribute the lack of research on community outcomes of service learning to theoretical and methodological problems, it is equally plausible that the neglect of community impact is a result of the biased focus on serving and changing students, which creates a self-perpetuating cycle.

This inequity in research focus might seem logical from the academic perspective, since faculty are rewarded, administrators are promoted, and funding is provided to both public and private institutions based on the satisfaction of their "customer base"—the student. Evaluations and assessments of almost every facet of academic progress are done, from accreditation self-studies, to program reviews, to conferences focusing on best practices, and so forth. And while those evaluations are increasingly asking institutions to document their community engagement, they are not yet asking them to document their community impact. As a result, the reporting of community service is done from within the institution rather than from outside of it. The consequence of this self-contemplation by institutions of higher education is that the voice of community organization staff and community members mostly goes unheard.

Given the lack of commitment to assessing service learning's impact on communities and community organizations, we feel compelled to ask the question: Who is served by service learning? The hallmark of an evolved view of higher learning is the willingness to look at issues from different angles with an open mind and change course where appropriate to ensure the sustainability of the practice. This volume seeks to at least partially redress the neglect of research on the community impact of service learning.

A Paucity of Past Research

We do not know much about community reactions to service learning. The little bit of research that is available concludes that community organizations are relatively satisfied with the service that they receive (Vernon and Ward, 1999; Ferrari and Worrall, 2000; Birdsall, 2005). For the most part, however, the research on satisfaction has remained at a relatively superficial level, using Likert Scale questionnaires or focus groups.

The lack of in-depth substantive research on the community impact of service learning is illustrated by the famous work of Cruz and Giles (2000) that found numerous claims regarding the benefits of service learning to the community, but little substantiation of those claims and no mention of the challenges. One of the few studies that focused in-depth on community perceptions of service learning, which also happened to be one of the rare rural studies done, surveyed sixty-five rural nonprofit organization directors and then conducted follow-up interviews with thirty of them. The research found that the directors were overwhelmingly pleased with their service learning outcomes. However, they also found that student schedules, short-term commitment, and training needs created challenges that were compounded by lack of communication with their supervising faculty (Vernon and Ward, 1999).

The issue of communication between community and academy also appears in other research by Birdsall (2005) and Jones (2003), and can be seen as an indicator of an important underlying problem with the service learning model that nonprofits may not have been asked about in earlier research. The lack of communication can be so profound that some organizations do not distinguish between service learning and community service (Birdsall, 2005), and they do not understand that service learning is supposedly connected to course content, learning objectives, and grading.

There is also some suggestion that there are important cultural differences between the community and academy. Bacon (2002), using separate focus groups of community organization staff and faculty, identified a cultural divide between those from the community and higher education sides of the relationship. In short, organization staff members are more willing to view themselves as learners, to link learning to action, and to see learning as a collective activity. Faculty seem more inclined to think of themselves as the experts—the keepers of the knowledge that they will impart to the students or the agencies with whom they are partnering (Bacon, 2002). This has important implications for how supervising faculty and community organizations communicate with each other. Jones (2003) argues that communities often are not recognized as having their own expertise to offer in the relationship. Could this be an academic prejudice toward PhD-holding faculty, and an assumption that anyone without an advanced degree running a nonprofit can't have a comparable amount of knowledge about his or her own work? Is that why community organization staff are asked to provide training and education for students without any remuneration for their time? Does that explain why professors still provide little to no training for students before sending them out to the community? And does that attitude bode well for a partnership where knowledge gained through experience with an issue is often more important than just reading about it?

These questions relate to the final theme we can glean from the miniscule body of literature on community reactions to service learning—concerns about the unequal relationship between community and academy. Jones (2003) suggests that much service learning will be initiated by the institutions, but the burden of managing the service learning students will fall disproportionately on the community organizations that host them. In fact, there is some reason to suspect that poor communities may be serving the students more than the students are serving the community (Sandy and Holland, 2006). The exception to this disparity in the balance of workload may be the community organizations that experience a more equal relationship with tribal, historically black, and Hispanic-serving colleges and universities (Ward and Wolf-Wendel, 2000).

Beyond this superficial indication that there may be communication, cultural, and power issues in service learning relationships, however, we know little about how service learning affects communities. We especially don't know how service learning affects communities from the perspective of those who live and work there. That puts us in dangerous territory. By not knowing what service learning does to the communities it purports to serve, we risk creating unintended side effects that exacerbate, rather than alleviate, the problems those communities suffer from. Furthermore, as academics, we risk burning bridges rather than building them if the communities decide our students are doing more harm than good, or are more trouble than they are worth. We may be setting into motion dialectical processes that ultimately undermine the entire effort of service learning.

The Dialectic of Service Learning

Our willful ignorance of the community impact and perceptions of service learning are part of what we might consider a dialectical process. Viewing service learning as a dialectical organizational process means seeing it not as a simple linear cause-and-effect process, but as a feedback process where the combined effects, many of them unintended, can ultimately undermine the original program (Benson, 1977, 1983). To think dialectically, consider an organization attempting to improve women's access to mammography. They believe that poor women aren't getting mammograms because the nearest mammography center is too far away, so they bring a portable mammography truck into the neighborhood once a month during the day. A year later, they look at the statistics on who is using the portable option and find out that the number of women from the neighborhood who are getting mammograms has not increased. In desperation, they go out and ask women why they aren't getting mammograms and discover it is because the truck is there only during the day when the women are working. They also learn that many women are quite irritated by the organizers' lack of sensitivity to their work schedules. Therefore, a program that was designed to both provide better medical service and build a better image of the medical profession is not affecting the former and is actually undermining the latter. A dialectical analysis then asks us to think about programmatic implementations as containing either latent or manifest contradictions that, left unresolved, can wreck the program itself.

To conduct a dialectical analysis, J. K. Benson (1977, 1983) directs us to look at the relationship between multiple programmatic goals, or between the goals and their implementation, which create outcomes that feed back into the program itself in potentially disruptive ways. People attempt to implement beliefs and principles in organizational settings, but they are never able to do so without constraint. Conditions that are not wholly compatible with the implementation are created by external funding and legal constraints and mandates, internal organizational structures and policies, and the informal power relations that exist within the organization and between the organization and its outside world. The lack of compatibility can subvert or divert the implementation in ways that participants neither intend nor recognize.

In service learning, the focus on student-learning goals, to the exclusion of any theoretical consideration of community development outcomes, has created a situation where we don't know what internal contradictions may be occurring. For example, we don't know the extent to which the development of service learning programs to primarily serve student and institutional interests may undermine community interests, which may negatively impact the community and undermine community support for the service learning program. If community input isn't solicited, it could come as a big surprise one day when faculty call "the usual suspects" in their community Rolodex, expecting to quickly and conveniently place a class of twenty students, and have the executive director just say, "No, thanks!" That has actually happened in many indigenous communities, as decades of exploitive research have led those communities to deny access to both researchers and students from higher education institutions (Smith, 1999). Randy Stoecker has a twenty-year history as a community-engaged academic, and has seen more bad than good service learning:

I have had so many scary experiences with service learning. The other day I was talking with a colleague who runs a service learning course. He encourages his students to think up projects and then go do them, arguing that it's not so important that the project succeed, but that the student learns something from it. I've heard other academics talk about the community as a "laboratory" where students try things. None of them reflect on the consequences for the community of failed projects, or faulty experiments. Indeed, none of them even develop a relationship with the communities in which their students are making their mistakes.

I must admit to some of this myself. The semester before this research project, I let my students search out their community projects. I always required a letter from the sponsoring agency at the beginning of the project agreeing to it, and one at the end stating that the student fulfilled their obligations. But I rarely had any relationship with the organization staff. This research has forced me to rethink all of that and to try some new things, in close collaboration with a community organization. Listening carefully to the organization staff, one thing I learned was how much time they put into supervising students. So we tried a model where one student would get trained as an intermediary and would supervise all the other service learning students. It didn't work perfectly, but it saved the organization about twenty hours in supervisory time and got some real work accomplished.

But the contradictions of the wrong way of producing civic engagement through higher education have become increasingly obvious as we have worked on this book. I've now encountered two students who have had their dissertations disrupted because the indigenous communities with which they were working decided that the benefits of the research were unfairly balanced in favor of the student and the institution. I have talked to a group of organizations in another small city who look with dread upon the annual spring ritual when the high schools empty and force all of their students to do community service that seems more like some kind of perverted work-release program than anything that has any benefit for anyone. Groups around the nation and indeed the world are beginning to speak up and decry what they see as a poorly considered theory of civic engagement in education today.

The unheard community organization voices, our partners in non-profit organizations and even ad hoc neighborhood grassroots groups who host service learners, are crucial to helping us conduct this dialectical analysis. But we must listen to them first. This project set out to listen carefully to those partners. Their voices speak quite clearly about the dialectical processes, and resultant contradictions, that may be undermining what we are trying to achieve.

A Way of Listening to Unheard Voices

How did we set out to learn what the staff of community organizations think about service learning? The process evolved gradually. I (Randy Stoecker) arrived in Madison, Wisconsin, in 2005 with an undeserved reputation as a service learning supporter (since I'd been criticizing the practice for at least half a decade by that time). I was escorted around town by a tireless community advocate and academic staff member at the University of Wisconsin named Margaret Nellis, who had been trying for even longer to guide the university toward truly serving communities in Madison through service learning. As we drove from organization to organization that day, we started hearing stories of some of the problems that community groups were having with service learning students. As I later met with more and more community groups, as part of an informal listening project, the weariness of organization staff who exhausted themselves trying to find make-work for students every semester became palpable.

After hearing too many stories of frustration with service learning, we started considering the possibility of doing something systematic to address this issue. Consequently, in November 2005, we convened a meeting of directors and volunteer coordinators who represented a diverse array of about twenty organizations to talk about service learning. The organization staff who attended the meeting were not uniformly negative about service learning; indeed, they actually liked the concept, but they were frustrated by its implementation in their organizations. When we asked whether they would like to start a process of really looking seriously at their concerns to see if we could do something about them, they said yes. Seven participants from that focus group agreed to form a core group to guide the research process. Our first decision was to focus on small- to medium-sized nongovernmental organizations (defined roughly as those with less than a $1 million annual budget and/or twelve or fewer full-time staff). School systems, government departments, and large nonprofits have more resources to risk, whereas small- to medium-sized organizations cannot afford to waste them on service learning that is not useful. In some ways, they also have the most to gain, as a few highly effective service learners can have a profound effect on the organization's capacity. It is important to understand that, while many of these organizations were part of the community fabric and were led by the constituencies they served, many others were traditional nonprofit organizations led by outside staff and boards. Our research, consequently, represents the reactions of those who are responsible for recruiting, training, managing, and evaluating service learners, not necessarily those who were subject to the services and projects in which the students were involved.

The next step was to put together a process to find out what community organizations really thought about service learning. For that we needed capacity, so with support from the University of Wisconsin's Morgridge Center for Public Service, the Edgewood College Human Issues Studies Program, and the Madison Area Technical College Volunteer Center, we recruited students to a special seminar on qualitative research methods billed as a community-based research course. We got eleven students, three university-based AmeriCorps°VISTA members, and an Edgewood College community partner specialist in human issues to participate in the seminar. Beth Tryon, the Edgewood staff member who has been working for three years with community partners facilitating service learning projects, is the coeditor of this project. Amy Hilgendorf, one of the AmeriCorps°VISTA members, also assisted with the editing of this volume.

The research presented in this book was designed jointly by the core community group (mostly executive directors and volunteer coordinators from social service and advocacy organizations), members of the student seminar, and two faculty researchers. We first held a brainstorming session to design the questions that would elicit the best information about their perceptions of service learning. Suggestions coming from the focus group were so fast and furious, we filled an entire wall of a large meeting room with notes on flip-chart paper! These ideas boiled down to a list of seven main questions. This group agreed to use a broad definition of service learning that included any student performing any service for credit. That included some students that may more accurately be considered interns or practicum students. We know there are many service learning purists who will object to this inclusion. The reality we discovered, however, is that there is very little service learning that conforms to narrow definitions and, from the community organization's perspective, hairsplitting academic definitions are so out of touch with the actual practice of service learning in community organizations that they are nearly irrelevant. In addition, adopting a broad definition allowed us to compare community organization staff reactions to different types of student placements. Here we actually found more variation in reaction between long-term and short-term service learning than we did between long-term service learning and placements such as internships, as we discuss in the chapter on short-term service learning.

We created a master list of small- and medium-sized nonprofit organizations that had worked with service learners from information obtained through the service learning offices at the three higher education institutions in Madison, and from other sources of the class members. We initially identified a population of 101 organizations that had worked with service learners from one or more institutions, though we have identified about twenty more organizations since this research. Madison is ripe with opportunity for study, as it claims the distinction of having the highest number of nonprofit organizations per capita in the United States, as well as a large number of activists and dedicated, interested community members. The organizations we contacted ranged from traditional social service groups to those dealing with worker's rights, women's advocacy, youth programs, and environmental issues. We divided up the list and made phone requests for a one-hour interview with the appropriate staff member at each organization. We targeted the staff member who had the most experience working with service learners, normally the executive director or volunteer coordinator, if they were fortunate enough to have one. Some organizations declined, based on their belief that they had been erroneously identified as having service learners. Others either had recently lost or rehired the volunteer coordinator or other staff person who managed service learning, and didn't feel like they had the capacity to participate. Most of those who declined cited time constraints. A small number initially agreed to be interviewed but then did not keep their appointments. This is all to be expected given that we were approaching the most vulnerable nonprofit organizations in the city. Those that we weren't able to interview didn't seem to change the representativeness of the sample. The final interviewees still came from a very wide array of different types of organizations. We ended up interviewing sixty-seven staff from sixty-four organizations, with each seminar participant doing five or six interviews apiece. We returned the transcripts to the interviewees for validity checks.

None of us had ever experienced a qualitative research project with this many people working together at the same time—with the objective being a written report by the end of that semester. But since we didn't know it "couldn't be done"—we did it! We began the drafting process in class, sharing interview experiences and beginning to identify general themes from the data. A Web site developed specifically with our needs in mind provided a password-protected space to post our written transcripts and audio files. We then could download the partial interview transcripts from the site and review the texts, confirming and adding to the themes discussed in class. Everyone compared the themes to their interview experiences and suggested changes in the theme structure. For example, one student found that many of his interviewees discussed various roles that service learning played in an organization, such as providing extra hands to accomplish the organization's regular work, adding new "bonus" capacity, or simply helping prepare future nonprofit professionals. Another student distinguished these discussions as describing "self versus altruistic motives" or "organization versus student benefits" and believed that the organization's orientation greatly influenced its subsequent decision making about such things as accepting service learners and evaluating their work. Because of this discussion, we reframed a theme on service learning definitions to highlight organizations' motivations and goals for service learning as well.

Through the iterative in-class and online discussions, seven themes emerged:

1. Goals and motivations of community organizations for service learning
2. Finding and selecting service learners
3. Structuring service learning
4. Managing service learners and service learning projects
5. Diversity and service learning
6. Relationship and communication with the higher education institutions
7. Indicators of success

These themes corresponded with, but did not completely mirror, the original questions we had about community reactions to service learning. Students then broke into two- or three-person teams and each team coded all the interviews for their major theme and analyzed all the interviews to develop that theme and specify subthemes, following the grounded theory approach (Glaser and Strauss, 1967). Each team took responsibility for crafting the findings from their theme into a chapter of the report. The grounded theory process and the openness of the interview protocol allowed issues to emerge that we had not been able to predict beforehand.

We made a conscious decision to include many of the richest quotes from the transcripts to illustrate the main points of each category, so that community organization reactions could be told as much as possible in the words of the community agency staff. We posted drafts of the report on a public Web site for community organization staff and anyone else who was interested to review and validate (Mays and Pope, 2000; Morse et al., 2002). The chapters you see in this collection are revisions of the original student team reports.

But we didn't want to stop with a report, so the end of the semester culminated in a "planning event" to which we invited all the agencies that had been contacted, even those that had been unable to participate in the interviews. Our class and about thirty community organizations gathered for approximately four hours in a large meeting room at the United Way building, with food, drink, and lots of markers and Post-it Notes. The event began with poster stations where each student group presented the main points of their chapter and agency staff could circulate and ask questions. The organization attendees each received a dot sticker to place on the poster of their choice to indicate the category they were interested in discussing further later in the day.

Before we held those small-group discussions, we split the attendees arbitrarily into two halves to form "fishbowls," where they listened to live interviews of two agency staff who'd had what they considered "nearly ideal" service learning experiences. These formed the basis of some ideas for recommendations for better practice. We then sorted ourselves into the small-group discussions, and asked the agency representatives to help devise a list of recommendations based on the report that would strengthen relationships between academic institutions and community agencies. There was a certain amount of overlap of recommendations from the small groups and the discussions strongly reinforced the research findings.

This experience gave us assurance that we were on the right track. The main suggestion from several of the small groups at the planning event was to create some type of document outlining a list of "Community Standards for Service Learning." So we embarked on another series of focus-group conversations with some of the organizations we interviewed, and other interested nonprofits. This culminated in a brochure that detailed the community's standards for service learning, and we are now seeking endorsements for the standards from both the community and the academic side across greater Madison.

We have been presenting our findings to everyone who would listen—at any gathering we can find of any combination of community organizations, faculty, students, and service learning professionals. We weren't sure how these community recommendations would be received by folks from the academic side. Would higher education administrators be defensive? Would faculty scoff at the suggestions, saying that there's no way they could follow them with all the other demands on their time? Would service learning professionals resist the implications for the structure of their programs? We found a surprising amount of support for these recommendations on the community side. As well, people on the academic side of the equation are excited and grateful to have this information, as they would like to improve their service learning practice. They approach us with the brochure clutched in their hands, thanking us for creating two succinct pages of basic principles, at which point we must confess it was our community organization partners who limited us to one sheet of paper.

We don't know where else this might take us next, but if we have helped even a few nonprofit agencies to feel more empowered in their work with service learning students, faculty, and administration, then the time has been well spent.

The Findings

Our primary objective in the initial research was a simple, comprehensible report for the community organizations to learn of our findings and from which they could craft an action project. However, after reading the drafts, we began to think that we had something pretty unique and important that might deserve a wider reading audience. We, and many of the organization staff we spoke with, wanted to tell the world what we found. What we learned about the insights of community organization staff concerning the current state of service learning was eye-opening, and we are convinced it will enlighten others as well.

Our research goes far beyond the paucity of current research on community reactions to service learning to take a much deeper look at how community organizations define, perceive, and evaluate service learning. In doing so, we diverge slightly from the seven themes that emerged from the research process. Organization representatives raised many provocative issues related to communication and relationship building, training and management of service learners, and cultural competency. But perhaps the most consistent theme that emerged was the frequent reference to challenges associated with short-term service learning. This was something we hadn't really been expecting and it was therefore all the more surprising, since this type of service learning is so prevalent. The complaints about it were so frequent that we have revised the structure of the original report to devote an entire chapter to the problem of short-term service learning.

The following chapters discuss the challenges, pitfalls, and praise of service learning from the viewpoint of the community. Those of you who have poured your hearts and souls into service learning may find this book a bit painful to read. The community organizations we spoke with have some strong critiques of service learning practices that have become all too typical in the new millennium. Some readers may reject our focus on the problems. In many cases, the problems we describe in this volume are often voiced by a minority of organizations, and it would be easy for someone to say that because only a sixth, or a third, of the organizations identify a problem that it's not a problem. Of course, in our country, it is always the minority that has been ignored. Often, that minority also represents the proverbial tip of the iceberg. Since we did not know what we would find, we did not have a checklist of specific problems. But we have spoken to organizations who have read our results and have said "me too," even when they didn't tell us that concern during the initial interview. Furthermore, a problem can be considered widespread if it is experienced by only a tenth of the organizations.

By the same token, every time we could gather enough positive information on a subject to consider it a subtheme, we included it. Our hope was to show things that *are* working for the community organizations so that those practices might be incorporated into future service learning project planning. The final chapter on indicators of success reinforces the emphasis of this book on improving, not undermining, service learning. Indeed, our conclusion, following a dialectical analysis, is that the greatest threat to the sustainability of service learning is to continue our current common practice.

We also want the reader to know that our collection of voices is incomplete. Because our focus was on the staff of community organizations who managed service learners, you only indirectly hear voices of community constituency members who receive services from service learners. This is consistent with the other research out there, and has the same shortcomings. Because we did not talk with community members impacted (or not) by service learning, one could argue that we do not know if the concerns expressed by community organization staff matter. Such a dismissal, however, would be shortsighted. Many of the negative impacts of the dominant model of service learning described by community organization staff are obvious to all who would listen. It is not the case that we can't judge the negative impacts of service learning from the voices of community organization staff, but only that we can't judge the extent of the negative impacts. At this point in the path of research on service learning, organization staff are the first stop. Such research defines the questions and issues that we can explore with more depth at the grassroots level. It can, in fact, be part of a conscientization process with community members to support their critical analysis of service learning as a next step toward removing the higher education dominance of the practice.

Beyond the goal of improving service learning, we feel a responsibility to promote the voices of our community partners, since they have long been marginalized in the service learning frenzy. With their lack of power over the institutions they deal with, and their need to be receptive to college-student volunteer help, it seems crucial to continue to work toward making service learning a smoother experience for them, and in that way to be doing some good in the community. When service learning is done right, with proper input from the agencies that are being served, it can be a most useful tool both for filling urgent needs in society and still fulfilling learning objectives, maybe in an even deeper way. Our hope is that our research may contribute to the dialogue between campus and community so that improvements are made in a timely enough fashion to mitigate some of the challenges straining the capacities of the nonprofit organizations that are gracious enough to allow learners into their daily work.

But now let us listen to the unheard voices of the community organization staff who host service learners.

Motivations of Community
Organizations for
Service Learning

Shannon M. Bell and Rebecca Carlson

When we consider the plight of small- and medium-size non-profits, stretched far beyond their capacity and watching the needs of their constituencies grow while the resource pie shrinks, it's easy to understand why they would accept service learners, even though this can bring extra duties for the organization staff. Organizations have mouths to feed, bodies to shelter, children to tutor, victims to protect, families to support, neighborhoods to restore, and all manner of other services to provide. And all of these jobs are far bigger than their small organizations. Many organizations attempt to recruit volunteers, but they are often so busy doing the work that they don't have time to find others to help them do it. All this makes service learners hard to pass up, even though some of them may not show up for more than one day.

But understanding the motivations of small- and medium-size community organization staff to host service learners is not that simple. Indeed, in some ways, the obvious explanation—that community organizations are motivated toward service learning to put more bodies into the work—is even wrong. The reasons that agency staff are motivated to work with college-student service learners go far beyond simple notions of "we couldn't survive without them." Their motivations are in fact quite complex, involving consideration not just of their own immediate organizational needs or those of the community they serve but also the long-term interests of society itself (Shaffett, 2002).

In this chapter, we first explore the differences between volunteers and service learners and the extent that such differences matter to community organizations. Then, we examine the complexities of nonprofit staff motives to work with service learners through a discussion of the different types of motives that respondents expressed. While we classify four types of motives here, many organizations declared more than one motive or overlapping motives. These four motives are:

- *The Altruistic Motive to Educate the Service Learner:* Agencies sometimes believe that part of their mission includes a responsibility to help students understand the issues facing their clients.
- *Long-Term Motives for the Sector and the Organization:* Some community organizations worry about the long-term support for their work. Who will be working at and donating to agencies and organizations like theirs?
- *The Capacity-Building Motive:* Organizations sometimes engage service learners to expand their organizational capacity.
- *The Higher Education Relationship Motive:* Some organizations take on service learners to build, strengthen, or preserve connections to colleges and universities.

Lastly, we discuss how community organization staff balance their concerns about service learning with their motivations to participate, and ultimately decide whether or not to be a service learning host.

Service Learners versus Volunteers

More than a decade ago, analysts (Bringle and Hatcher, 1996; Sigmon, Hemesath, and Witte, 1996) expressed concern that community organizations may not know the difference between student service learners and volunteers. Today, it appears, the situation is little different. Many of the community organization staff we spoke with did not have a very deep understanding of service learning, and some didn't even know if the students under their supervision were receiving course credit. Given the communication gaps between academy and community that characterize much service learning (Bringle and Hatcher 2002; Bender, 1993), it's hard for many agencies to know what flavor of volunteer they are dealing with. At any rate, service learners are an essential source of volunteers for some organizations' activities:

> We could not do all of the things we need to do without volunteers, and students are our primary volunteer base.

To the extent that a professor or student does not communicate learning goals to the organization, the organization will default to treating them as a volunteer and, in all likelihood, the student will act like a volunteer. Indeed, sixteen of the organization staff defined the work that service learners do as being the same or similar to the work done by their volunteers, even when they are given the option to do different and more advanced work. In many ways, volunteers do share characteristics with service learners, including common motivations such as a desire to help others, interest in the activity, a motivation to learn and gain experience, or a devotion to a cause (Lynch and McCurley, 1999). According to Millie Gore (2007), the only real difference in motivation between traditional volunteers and service learners is that of fulfilling a class requirement.

To what extent does a delineation between service learners and other volunteers make a difference? Interestingly, volunteers and service learners seem to exhibit the same shortcomings: lack of consistency and reliability, poor-quality work, lack of staff capacity to supervise, and so forth (Batenburg, 1995; Gazley and Brudney, 2005). But a significant difference between service learners and volunteers, especially in the eyes of the higher education institution, is the loss of opportunities to attend to the curricular goals of the service learner when they are treated as a volunteer. If students are recognized as volunteers but not service learners, their involvement is often limited to activities that only match their current abilities and do not stretch them in ways that will meet their educational objectives.

By contrast, where course goals are a larger and more explicit part of the service learning relationship, students sometimes participate in more complex activities, such as the administrative functions of the organization. They work with directors, attend staff meetings, and participate in other sorts of higher-level work. Overall, it seems the more explicit the service learning goals, the more structured the educational experience:

> I think one of the things that tends to be different is often they have some type of learning objectives, contract, or agreement that we talk about at the beginning . . . about exactly what type of things they are going to do and what they are going to learn, and there is often some midpoint check-in, and in the end there is often some reflection on their part.

Indeed, some organization staff who distinguished service learners from volunteers sometimes viewed their relationship with the individual in an entirely different way:

> I do think that service learning programs differ from volunteering in that volunteering is more task oriented. Service learning programs seem to be more a collaboration between the students and the organization.

Organization staff also highlighted unique qualities that students bring to the organization compared to traditional volunteers, as these two interviewees present:

> I think that the energy is just the moving force. The college volunteers, they have an energy and an outlook that is completely different from other volunteers. I think it's something that's contagious.

> I think that's why the college students are such a good fit for our program; they can relate better, they can establish a relationship in trust faster [with their young clientele]. The college student has really been our key solution.

Service learners who could also commit to longer periods of service were sometimes involved in specialized projects such as doing "a lot of analyses, research, help[ing] write narrative reports, [and] qualitative and quantitative reports," or observing "the process and the board of directors." Work-study students or interns, in particular, were "placed in a more employee-type role, and have more responsibility" than a more short-term service learner or a volunteer. (See Chapter 4 for more discussion of short-term service learning.)

The Altruistic Motive to Educate the Service Learner

We were greatly surprised to learn that many community organizations hosted service learners not because it expanded organizational capacity, but because the organization staff saw it as part of their mission to educate the public, and considered students to be part of that public. Many community organization representatives explained that part of their motivation to host service learners was to teach them something. On occasion, that "something" was left undefined or defined through a generalized knowledge base such as, "I want them to be able to walk away with gaining some sort of skill from us." This is not a completely unique finding, as Sandy and Holland (2006: 34) also identified "the community partner's profound dedication to educating college students—even when this is not an expectation, part of their job description, or . . . provides few benefits for their organization" as a prime motivator for organization staff taking on service learners. But we were struck by how common this motivation was.

Community organization staff have a real motivation to teach service learners about how to pursue a cause in a real community context—getting students out of the classroom and away from textbooks to see the real world of specific social, environmental, economic, and educational issues. Some organization staff even believe this to be part of their mission:

> I believe it helps [the service learning students] put a face to the disease, in working with clients. I believe part of our mission, of course, is education and prevention, and by virtue of being around all this and going through the trainings and the orientation, they learn more about [the organization's cause].

Even when the staff person's expectation of the student is low, they still see value in using the service learning relationship as a means of fulfilling their broader educational mission:

What you have is an undergraduate student who needs to be introduced to a population or an issue, and they're not going to have this kind of investment and time . . . I think just hanging out here in this agency in the building and spending time is eye-opening.

Twenty-seven of the organizations interviewed expressed a motivation to teach the service learner about what it takes to work and do projects in community organizations. Organization staff, as illustrated by the next quotes, understand that most students have had very little exposure to the nonprofit world in academia, and service learning provides an avenue to achieve that exposure:

[O]ne of the reasons why I am so supportive of service learning programs [is] because they expose students to nonprofit organizations beyond just volunteering, but get the students to think that "this could actually be a career path for me." A lot of students, especially at that age, want to do something good for the world, but then they get to the reality of looking for a job and they don't know how to connect their skills and interests to the nonprofit world. Nonprofits are just not something they are exposed to as possible careers.

It's a way to let someone see what your organization does and why it's important but it's also a really valuable experience for the student to be able to learn by doing and to be able to really be immersed in something and see how it works. I mean, we can sit here and talk about how [this organization] works, but you can only get a very limited idea of what actually happens here. So I can see how it's really valuable for the students.

And, once again, we see that the motivation to serve the student is so high that the organization will risk a low short-term return on their time investment, having students just "help out" rather than expecting highly skilled capacity assistance:

With the relationship we have right now, the [service] learning is more of an observational process. If you [the student] are interested in how a grassroots statewide network functions and how it can function pretty well, it's good to have the students come in and ask questions and observe that process. And then the service part is to just have them help with whatever is going on.

Long-Term Motives for the Sector and the Organization

Another value in giving service learners a hands-on experience in community organizations is to provide the community with graduates who come out of their program with a community competency of sorts. While many organizations think about service learners as part of a broad effort to impact society, others think of them more narrowly as future staff members for the nonprofit sector. This long-term perspective doesn't mean all staff expect students to return to their organization, but rather to support nonprofit work somewhere.

There are a number of community organization staff members who are concerned about ensuring the health of the nonprofit world into the future. They want to guarantee that there will be strong nonprofit professionals to one day take over their roles, as described by these three staff members:

As an agency, we are very committed to education. Not only are we committed to the work we do . . . but there's a large opportunity to educate, not only the patients and families and the community we work with but those people who hopefully will go out and do that sort of work.

But we are also doing it because we are wanting to further those programs as well. I want to personally make sure we have good social workers out there. I like supervising social-work students and furthering my field. I think that the other direct-service staff feel the same way when they get students in from their field.

We kind of just immerse them in the fire. . . . To me, the most valuable experiences are putting them into the situation because they are going to have to do that when they get out there. . . . Sink or swim.

Many nonprofit staff members have to take a long-term perspective to stay involved in service learning because, at least in the short run, service learning seems to be a net loss in terms of time and service:

> Just because a service learner comes in here today and doesn't set the world on fire, doesn't mean that the information they gained, the education they gain here, doesn't change them dramatically ten years from now or fifteen years from now. So, in some sense, we have to take a longer view of our role. Frankly, if we were going to look at what a service learner gives us, or gives to our clients, we would never do this. There's more to it than that . . . because someone's got to be doing this work twenty years from now.

Three interview participants had experienced service learning as students themselves and saw the experience as deepening their interest in nonprofit work. All noted that their motivation for hosting service learning came from, or at least was influenced by, their personal experience as a service learner or a volunteer prior to their work in a community-based organization:

> I had been a work-study student myself in the past—when I was getting my master's degree I had several different work-studies . . . so I learned. I had firsthand experience of how great from the student's perspective it can be to do that because you get to make contact and you get the professional experience. So I had that background.

One hope of the organization staff we interviewed is that the service learning experience in the real world results in a win-win situation—where the organization benefits, the community benefits, and the student benefits in the long-term scheme of hosting a service learner:

> It's an opportunity for people to develop some work-related experience that may be useful to them, but then it also has a benefit for the nonprofit organization ourselves, because we have limited resources, or to the people that we serve. So, it's one of those things that benefits everyone involved, I think.

Indeed, there are also organization staff who have a strong interest in educating students with hopes they will return as employees to the very organization where they were a service learner:

> Part of the reason we obviously have student learners is that they are really useful to us, but a huge piece of it is also that if we are going to continue doing what we are doing, we have got to train . . . the next generation of leaders. . . . I think it is really important that we are finding those students who want to learn how to do this kind of stuff, and teaching them and sort of nurturing them along, so when they graduate they have options in this field. Three of the staff here were people I had personally worked with when they were students, and when they graduated they came and started working here. So it is definitely, to me, the way to kind of make sure what we are doing is sustainable.

Community organization staff often see service learning as offering the potential for keeping students engaged as volunteers or employees after the formal service learning appointment concludes, a motivation not often taken into account in the design of service learning programs (Birdsall, 2005). Community agencies perhaps are willing to overlook a host of logistical hassles and other negative aspects of the arrangement in hopes that they are essentially training a long-term volunteer or potential future staff person.

The Capacity-Enhancing Motive

Altruistic and long-term interests notwithstanding, a prime motivator of our pool of community organizations to host service learners is their need for the services that students can provide (Tiamiyu and Bailey, 2001). Nearly everyone mentioned that the service itself is one of the essential goals of service learning. However, the duties that they expected students to provide varied.

One of the service goals highlighted by organizations is that service learners should contribute to the organization by working with their clientele in various capacities. Almost all of the organizations that provide direct services mentioned that serving the clientele is one of their goals for service learning because their "first and foremost priority is making sure someone gets served in the community" and that "the direct-service component is really important to understanding what [the organization is] doing." Some direct-service organizations used students to keep the ratio of staff-to-clientele lower, especially in many of the organizations that work with children. A handful of direct-service organizations commented on the appeal of students working with clientele because it provides a closer relationship to the organization and may also provide a more satisfying service learning experience:

> It also helps to make a stronger volunteer-to-program connection, volunteer-to-clientele connection. . . . You can tell that [they're] really involved in the class and I think that helps [them] to grow and give volunteer satisfaction . . . versus having them come and say, "Well, today we have this office project for you to do," if that's not something they're into.

> I like to think that when I bring people into my program and into my clients' lives that they have a meaningful role.

A theme we see in later chapters, however, is that a number of direct-service organizations did not feel comfortable having service learners working directly with their clients. Many organizations provide critical assistance to at-risk individuals, requiring a lot of experience and training, and an untrained student working in that capacity is not a good fit for their organization. In addition, a number of organizations have difficulty finding service learners with the commitment that would allow them to reliably provide direct client services. Because the impacts of service learners on those who receive their services are not carefully evaluated, and there is a lack of resources to support such data gathering, agency staff must rely only on their own perceptions, rather than those of community members, to guide their use of service learners. Not knowing whether service learners provide benefit or harm can make organization staff hesitant to deploy them in sensitive situations.

While some organization staff are reluctant to use service learners in direct service, they still want the students to receive a quality educational experience and find other ways that service learners can expand their organizational capacity. Outreach, whether for fund-raising or broader community education, is typically an important part of a community organization's program, and many of them engage service learners in their outreach activities. One group of interviewees, for example, wanted to teach students about their organization and get them enthused about its mission in hopes the students would help promote the organization's image in the broader community. Outreach can start off by reaching out to the service learners themselves:

> We are trying to get our staff to do more outreach, because they can pitch [their programs] and educate people more about their programs than I can. And they have the time to focus more on a certain class or professor at the schools and they have had better luck that way.

When that strategy succeeds, it can then lead to broader community outreach, as these three interviewees explain:

> [W]e were able to get students excited about the work that we were doing, sort of spread the word in whatever way you can spread the word, you know? I think that's a really great thing.

> We benefit in a lot of ways. Like I said, the interactions; just having kids get exposure to different people. We benefit because [the service learners] take the good word out about [the organization] . . . you can't pay for that kind of good word, you know.

> Our outcomes would be to have another advocate for . . . the work that we do that is in the public. . . . That is one of the goals we have—we describe it as building a fan club base that understands and promotes our work.

Another way organizations engage service learners to expand capacity is to have them work on projects that the agency does not have the capacity or the skills to do. This project-based service learning model, where a student enters the organization not just to volunteer but also to accomplish a specific project, is becoming increasingly popular. Whether it is a Web site, a database, a survey, or support for a specific community event, project-based service learning is viewed as a way to maximize the energy of the student and expand the capacity of the community organization (Chamberlain, 2003; Draper, 2004; Coyle, Jamieson, and Oakes, 2005). Project-based service learning is also a means of managing the problem of short-term service learning, and we discuss in Chapter 4 the specific ways to implement the model.

Community organization staff are motivated to use project-based service learning as a way to get their work done and to tap into specific strengths and skills of students. Eighteen of the sixty-four organizations we interviewed highlighted contributions made by service learners that ranged from an "intern taking on a big project the organization has always wanted to do" to working on Web sites and other projects that the organization does not have the skills for, noting that "students add new energy, new ideas, creativity; they keep [the organization] rolling forward with stuff." Many of those organizations commented that "one of the things that [organization staff] like about the service learning programs is that they tend to draw from different disciplines" and thus "college students come with a lot of great skills, a lot of different ways of looking at things" that the organization would otherwise lack:

> The learning curve for us, this is something that we have no idea what to do or how to do it. We look to the students for some guidance—you know, you learn it, tell us—rather than us learning it, because of that kind of time commitment.

> Because you have that many people, you also have that many brains, that many people with ideas, that many people with energy, with drive, with different backgrounds, that can come in and say, "Did you ever think about doing this?" We have done awesome things because students have come in and said, "I would like to try this," "I know about this, I know about that."

A couple of organization staff members said that they preferred service learners who presented a relevant project idea to them because then they would not have to expend the resources to create something for the service learner to do. Not just any project will do, however. There has to be a true fit between what the student proposes and what the organization needs:

Where it has worked best is when a student comes in with a project or activity that really fits with what our organization is doing . . . things we've always wanted to do that a student wants to do for a class that brings stuff in that we haven't had the capacity to do.

Most interviewees indicated that they wanted to balance both student and organization needs, though not at the cost of the organization's ultimate mission. One organization staff member connected project-based service learning with the longer-term educational goals discussed earlier:

I think education would be way better if more project-based learning went on, and maybe service learning is the epitome of project-based learning—because there's something so good about having a tangible benefit to somebody that . . . it elicits energy from people to make something happen.

Nearly two-thirds of the organizations we interviewed had students working on preestablished programs or projects as a way to expand their capacity. About one-third discussed having students work on new, or nonroutine, projects. These projects generally take more time to develop, a luxury not all nonprofits have.

Because we have a smaller staff and because hours are desperately short in terms of the amount of things there are to do versus the time to do them, I really try not to create work for students to do. I want them to do work that's already here. . . . I've found that in the past when we made the project up to fit what they needed, neither of us was particularly successful . . . they didn't feel like they'd achieved what they wanted to do and all I felt like I was doing was babysitting or answering questions or whatever.

Sometimes organization staff have a "wish list" that students can plug right into, but that is often not the case.

We tend not to have projects sitting around for them, and tend not to have the time or energy to create projects that are going to be meaningful for them. . . . It's just too hard to come up with things that can sit around and wait until they would meet somebody's service learning goals and yet are something that we need.

Some organizations find that even project-based service learning entails some risk, particularly when they don't have a comfortable service learning relationship to begin with:

Service learners probably are more useful for [the] things we want to get done category versus need to get done. Ultimately, you want to control your own destiny and to [not] put that dependence into something you are not quite sure would work well. As a nonprofit organization without lots of service learning experiences, you are probably not going to take those sorts of risks.

A couple of other organizations commented that proposed projects worked less well if they fit the needs of the student better than the needs of the organization, which remains an issue in project-based service learning (Bradford, 2005).

There is a tension even in project-based service learning, then, where we can see the service learning dialectic at work. The relationship may reinforce expert-client thinking in the student's mind, rather than promote a partnership philosophy (Joint Educational Project, n.d.) where the student realizes he or she is also benefiting from the experience. To manage this dialectic, one organization staff member felt it was important to "make sure that we have meaningful projects that are going to satisfy both the volunteers' or service learners' requirements as well as do something really good for the organization." One organization representative described a strategy to negotiate those different interests:

It was sort of an iterative process of, "Okay, your project has to incorporate certain things for you. We'd like to get certain things done." You sort of iterate until you define something that's good for everybody.

Going through this negotiation process, as we discuss in later chapters, is for neither the casual service learner nor the casual service learning host. Thus, organization staff look for dedicated faculty with whom they can build relationships to help ensure access to qualified and committed students.

The Higher Education Relationship Motive

Community organizations can access much more than student labor from higher education institutions. If they can find it, some community groups make good use of research support, technical assistance, training, and various kinds of specialized knowledge. Indeed, community-based research continues to gain in popularity as a form of partnership between the community and higher education that is more focused and community-driven than service learning (Strand et al., 2003). As higher education institutions reach out to their surrounding communities, however clumsily, at least some area organizations are taking them up on the offer.

In our research, fourteen organization representatives spoke of underlying connections to the higher education institutions in Madison, Wisconsin. With a flagship state university, a faith-based private college, and a community college in a city of just over 200,000 people, there are a lot of intellectual resources. The desire to build and sustain relationships with these institutions is a motivating factor of some organizations to host service learners, anticipating that the relationship will lead to connections to professors, courses, and the latest research in the organization's specific field:

> Working with students sometimes helps create new links with faculty members and helps to just get our name out there, too.

> [The service learners are] able to bring some of the materials that they're learning, more in terms of, "Oh, we just studied that in this course that I was taking and this has really been helpful" or "I'm going to be taking this course next semester and this is giving me some perspective that's really going to help in this next class." And I just love that kind of synchronicity of it all and I think that's really important.

As we discuss in later chapters, organizations also do not want to be left out of possible access to resources. So, in many cases, they will accept service learning as the price of continued entry to other—sometimes more valuable—higher education resources. We heard a number of organization staff express concern that if they turned down offers of service learners, they could be taken off the list and might not hear of other future offers. There is a power dynamic between higher education institutions and community organizations similar to that between any resource provider and recipient. The resource provider controls the resources, and the community organization staff have to figure out how to get the most useful resources from the provider. The difference, in this case, is that most funders and other resource providers don't freely offer resources—the organization has to apply for them. But in the case of higher education offers of service learning, it is more like a shell game where no one is sure of the prize. Will the best service learners come from class A or class B? Will accepting service learners from class C open the door to valuable future research support?

The dialectic of service learning, then, can set up an unhealthy relationship between organization and institution. As institutions try to maximize the learning opportunities for their students, and as organizations try to maximize their capacity to impact their communities, there is as much tendency to withhold information as there is to build strong relationships. It is not necessarily in the institution's interest to support the desire of community organization staff to host only the most highly skilled and productive students. Likewise, organization staff must balance accepting any student at any skill level with appearing to be too picky, which would potentially lead institutions to withhold information on individual students. A system that depends on the quality of the relationships underpinning it can be disrupted by underlying power inequalities.

How Motivations Influence Choices

Given some of the cautions identified above, how do community organizations decide how much risk to take on with service learning? How do they balance their needs and risks? For example, should they put the students in charge of essential services or restrict them to menial tasks? How much should they emphasize the long-term goals of creating a more educated student body compared to making sure they don't risk their organizational capacity?

Some organization staff discussed their own quandaries when trying to decide whether to take on service learners to provide routine, monotonous service (such as stuffing envelopes) or to participate in service that was more crucial to the organization and interesting to the student. Oftentimes, their decisions related to their definition of service learning and their motivation to engage the student. Other times, their decision to host service learners depended on the type of student and how much time the student could give. For example, when organizations hosted students doing an internship of up to ten or fifteen hours a week, they were often willing to assign more complicated tasks than they would for an average short-term (twenty-hour per semester) service learner. Indeed, organization staff preferred to offer deeper experiences to students, and thus desired longer-term commitments, as these three interviewees state:

> My ideal would be students working on a project that was more an integral part of what we are doing . . . and in order for that to happen, we will need a longer timeline in the semester.

> There's not much that people can do here that is meaningful that doesn't require an investment of time . . . there's always photocopying or some such, but making it an educational experience, it's a challenge for us.

> The amount of time committed by a student is directly related to the types of activities they are given. . . . The interns, we usually give them more of a role in the program and that is because we know that we have them for the whole semester or maybe the whole school year.

Others look at the relationship more from the perspective of the organization's needs, which often entwines both menial and more interesting tasks in order to really support the capacity needs of the organization:

Maybe they thought it was going to be more academic versus man-powered and then they are not happy. . . . You can be working on a report and then take the garbage to the curb. You kind of do whatever needs to get done and we expect the same thing from our volunteers.

But there are more variables than just time and organizational needs involved here. For at least one organization, having a student participate in other than menial tasks meant limiting the number of service learners:

I am very careful about the number of volunteers that come in here, because I don't want volunteers to come in and just sit. I want them to be able to come in and work with families and that means being very controlling about the number of volunteers that we have so that there aren't too many. . . . Staff were using volunteers inappropriately; they were having them fetch them lunch or have them doing their copying or their filing—just all their grunt work—and I told them that was not acceptable anymore.

Another staff member emphasized the need to treat one's loyal and long-standing volunteer corps with respect and fairness since they come to the organization with only an intrinsic motivation to help and not from a requirement for course credit:

Service learning with structured expectations, they [the students] get the cream of the volunteer opportunities because their programs require it, which seems unfair to the others, and the other people get stuck doing just the photocopies and the crap. . . . You want people who've been around awhile that have demonstrated that they're capable—you want to trust them with the more significant things because you've got confidence in them—whereas somebody who walks through the door, maybe they shouldn't get the fun stuff . . . and the things that have more impact. . . . By the time you figure out whether this person is going to follow through, it can often be too late, and there are a certain number every year that just bail on us.

These community organization staff seem to suggest a belief that effectively structuring service learning projects, increasing the length of service, recruiting the appropriate type of student, and having adequate agency capacity will produce the most successful service learning outcomes.

Conclusion

Reading some of the interviewee's comments could lead one to question why the community organizations would even bother with service learning—why not just keep using "plain old" volunteers? But it helps to keep in mind that many agency staff feel strongly that they are the ones providing a service, or that the arrangement is at least reciprocal. They get some crucially needed help with their programs and activities, but they also are using service learning to impart the mission of the organization to a relatively young, fresh, future workforce—people who will in only a few years be driving decisions about the environment, social justice, and other important issues.

Even against a backdrop of challenges presented by working with college students for course credit, the arrangement often makes sense for many organizations. In other cases, the incongruities may not be worth the time and effort needed to justify the relationship. It would be a good idea to examine the motivations of both partners—the institution and its faculty and student representatives, and the community organization—and make sure the goals of each are compatible before moving forward with a service learning project. Our upcoming chapters detail some crucial findings of the research that show the resultant trapdoors and land mines that lay in the path of service learning that truly serves communities, and provide clues that may help both educational institutions and community organizations think through their reasons for pursuing relationships and their strategies for building them.

3 Finding the Best Fit

How Organizations Select Service Learners

CASSANDRA GARCIA, SARAH NEHRLING,
AMY MARTIN, AND KRISTY SEBLONKA

Given the combined motives of community organization staff to both educate service learners and expand services to the community, how does a community organization find and recruit students who fit the bill? We know amazingly little about this question. Perhaps we have not considered the community's role in recruiting and selecting service learners because students historically have been recruited on the college campus and presented to the agencies. In this research, however, the organization staff were as likely to seek out students as they were to simply receive them. And the people we spoke to had plenty to say about the techniques, logistics, and various pros and cons of recruiting and choosing service learners to work with. Some of their comments and concerns presented here overlap with the themes of communication (detailed in Chapter 6) and expectations (a running theme throughout this volume and also described in Chapter 5). But in terms of the nuts and bolts of "how to get people in here to do stuff" at nonprofit agencies, there are a few distinct issues that deserve consideration in a separate space through a distinct lens. The issues we consider here are:

- *Making the First Contact:* How to develop the connections that lead to good service learning relationships.

- *Selecting and Placing Service Learners:* What criteria to use in choosing who to host and what to host them for.
- *Preferred Service Learner Characteristics:* What skills and attitudes characterize the best service learner?
- *The Role of Organizations' Expectations in Selecting Service Learners:* How a match between what the organization staff want and what students can provide influences service learning placements.

Making the First Contact

The first step in any service learning experience is making the initial connections among the organization, the professor, and the student. This can be initiated by any one or a combination of the three, and can happen through many different mediums (Bringle and Hatcher, 2002; Jacoby, 1996; Mihalynuk and Seifer, 2008; Pribbenow, 2002).

For nine of the sixty-seven organizations, the professor made the first contact. Organization staff explained that "professors contact us because students want a place they can speak Spanish," or maybe "the professor lets us know who she thinks are the best students and we bring them in for interviews." Sometimes, as two organizations mentioned, the professor recommends a student to an organization or "pitches us on a student." Many organization staff welcome this faculty-initiated contact. An alternate approach is for students to make the first contact with the organization, as was the case for another nine interviewees. Some organization staff, although happy to have students, are befuddled as to how the student learned about them:

> It was really interesting because this particular student sought us out. I was surprised when she contacted us and asked us to be our intern. She knew about [our organization], but I didn't know where the information had come from; we must have been on some resource list or I really don't know. She sought us out and said, "I would really like to work with you."

The third situation is when organization staff actively recruit students. There is some advice on recruiting volunteers or service learners written from various professional perspectives (Network for Good,

2007; McCurley and Lynch, 1989) as "how-to" guides to help nonprofits, but virtually no information on how community agencies say they
are presently doing it. Web site databases are mentioned as useful recruitment tools, which is more prominent in urban areas such as Madison, Wisconsin, through volunteeryourtime.org. The distinction here
is that the term "service learning" isn't a keyword, or even mentioned
on many of these Web sites. So the distinction between service learners and the regular volunteer cadre is invisible to an agency visiting or
posting on the site, and sometimes they have no way to document where
a particular volunteer is coming from. The National Service Learning
Clearinghouse has many detailed articles about how faculty recruit service learners, or how umbrella organizations like Learn and Serve
America recruit volunteers. Bringle and Hatcher (2002) have mentioned this issue from the community perspective. So this is a hit-and-
miss method of finding students, even in places where there are many
Web-based options. The challenges can be compounded in smaller
towns that have less options for searching out students or making their
needs known (Stoecker and Schmidt, 2008). In our research, we found
that organizations approach recruitment through three identified
strategies:

1. Attending volunteer fairs
2. Talking with classes and/or professors of certain classes
3. Using service learning centers and Web sites that post
   service learning opportunities

Community organization reactions to volunteer fairs were interesting. Some of the organizations that had staff members sit at volunteer
fair booths suggested that this activity allowed them to present their
programs to a wide audience all at once and keep current on the higher
education institutions' service learning programs. But the majority of
interviewees who discussed participating in volunteer fairs did not see
them as efficient, since the large amount of time spent staffing a booth
rarely produced new service learning recruits. Volunteer fairs were
especially problematic for small agencies that really couldn't afford the
time away from daily operations for a minimal return. To add insult to
injury, some institutions charge a booth fee, which could mean that a
nonprofit might actually come out behind if no one signs up to volun-

teer with them. Even if the organization doesn't have to buy booth space, the time commitment can be a net loss:

> We've taken part in the . . . volunteer days where you can go in and sit at a booth and talk to students . . . but if you sit there all day and end up with one volunteer, it's hard to justify that [use of time].

Volunteer fairs also tend to lump service learning and volunteer activities together, so in some cases agencies don't know whether a student's goal is to complete civic engagement for course credit.

Other organization staff look to take a bit more control over the situation by making the first contact with either a class whose topic is relevant to their work or a professor in a discipline compatible with their needs. They will make the first move to find out what field might be suitable and then work to find an instructor who is amenable to the idea of allowing an in-class presentation:

> Generally, they are in some type of class that has a connection to an issue here: poverty, class issues, [or] education. We rarely get volunteers who have nothing to do with the issues.

> If our work has some interest or something to offer students or professors whose classes they might be coming from . . . I try to find out what that connection really is and to make that work.

One organization staff person sums up the effects of visiting a class by saying that, after presenting to the class, "everyone is always intrigued and wants to do their student teaching or internship with us."

Sometimes it is difficult to determine who made the first contact (the professor, the student, or the organization) because a number of first contacts are made through relatively informal connections or even simply through word of mouth. But this can be a hit-and-miss proposition. While some interview participants talked about how students spread the word about their organization, others felt that "the momentum [is not] carried through from the student side of things."

Stronger relationships seem to work better for recruiting students. Three organizations mentioned using their personal connections, and about twelve said they rely on professional connections—often professors they already know—to jump-start service learning involvement in their organization. Three more organizations said they had firmly established contacts with professors at a higher education institution because staff within the organization were alumni of that institution. Others stressed the fact that the longevity of a relationship only strengthened their ties: "One school has been sending students to [our organization] so long, and they know what we have to offer, and it is a good fit for them."

The timing of the first contact, in whatever form, is crucial. Organization staff agree that the contact should be made early on, preferably before the semester begins (Peacock, Bradley, and Shenk, 2001). They also encourage students and possibly the faculty to be energetic in establishing a relationship with the organization:

> Students need to realize that nonprofits are working on limited resources and that it is really better to call ahead and to plan ahead. . . . Make sure that the students know that it is good to be assertive—send an application in, make the call, find out what is going on, and that will be very helpful.

Of course, it is also helpful for that initial contact to have some depth and structure. Otherwise, some community organization staff may wonder if they are wasting valuable time:

> Usually, for some reason, every single [course] requires that they interview the director about our program and our funding sources . . . [laughing] I'm tempted to videotape it and just plug it in for them!

This preterm contact is recommended in service learning manuals (Cress et al., 2005; Campus Compact, 2003), but many of our organizations gave the impression that they believe few faculty or students read those manuals. A number of organizations, especially those who need to do a background check on every volunteer they utilize, expressed frustration when "someone [calls] on Friday and says, 'Oh, I'd like to be a tutor,' and they need something signed by Monday saying they're going to be placed." Agencies also said that they do not appreciate it when someone "come[s] in the third week of February saying, 'I need seventy hours by April.'" This puts an unfair burden on the organization to restructure volunteer opportunities to fit the student's needs, if they want to have that help at all.

On the other hand, a few organizations said they themselves were the cause of missed opportunities because they did not get their requests for service learners out early enough, and lacked adequate planning and recruitment on their side:

> As far as recruiting volunteers and service learners, we don't really have anything formal right now. I'm trying to do a little volunteer coordination, but I don't really have a lot of time for it. . . . I've sent some volunteering queries, but no one has taken me up on it. I think I need to get into classrooms and make a pitch or something and take the time to be over there personally because e-mail is just not doing it right now.

Most important, a number of our organizations had not developed a specific strategy for recruiting and using service learners; often because they were too busy just doing the day-to-day work of the organization. Developing a service learning plan and actively recruiting students is a luxury for which too few organizations have the capacity. Organizations that are farther away from the higher education institutions need to recruit especially hard, as students will more likely want to fill their service obligations as conveniently close to campus as possible. This can be especially burdensome for rural organizations, but the challenge is present even for those organizations that may just be a few miles from campus.

Selecting and Placing Service Learners

Once the organization gets in contact with a student, the selection and placement process begins. Some of these organizations start from the position that they will not "just accept whoever is available." Almost half of our interviewees mentioned holding interviews with prospective service learning students, and some even do a follow-up interview to make sure the organization and student fit well with each other. Others use a more orientation-style interview, where organization staff "arrange a meeting with them and get to know them; tell them about our organization and find out in a more holistic sense what they are about."

The range of selectivity varies among organizations, sometimes because they need only a certain number of volunteers. One agency staff person justified their selectivity by saying that "when you have too many volunteers, there will be one or two who do a really good job and there will be one or two that just sit around and do nothing." Another nonprofit representative explained that "it's sort of that fine line between being really beneficial to the student and the organization and kind of failing for both the organization and the students." Some organization staff are "very selective" in choosing service learners, setting aside any fears that their high standards may alienate those who provide the students. Conversely, along with having a plethora of nonprofits in this city, at least one-fifth of the population is college students, a likely target for volunteer recruiting:

> I have worked with other organizations and they have a real crisis or panic mind-set, like whenever volunteers come in the door we have to take them because we won't get more, and I am really of the exact opposite mind-set. This is Madison, Wisconsin. If there is anyplace with an abundance of volunteers. . . . It is our goal to make our volunteer program as volunteer-friendly as possible, but at the same time, we don't need to take an inappropriate volunteer or a bad match because there is always someone else that will step up and take their place.

Other agencies just require that potential service learners have passed a background check and are in moral agreement with their mission. Finally, there are organizations that do not turn any students away. They are "willing to take anybody willing to do it."

Approximately twenty of the interviewees said they try to place students in activities that fit the students' interests. They generally attempt to determine those interests either during an interview or through casual conversation. A few organizations mentioned receiving letters of interest from students, and they wished more students would submit such letters. One interviewee also noted that writing a letter of interest prepares students for writing application cover letters. A few organizations have encountered students who specify certain experiences or client contact, such as:

> For certain types of children—Special Ed, ESL, a wide range of different types . . . it runs the gamut. If we know about what people are looking for, almost all of the time we can accommodate them."

And while some organizations find themselves in a position to select among several service learning prospects, other organizations must compete with each other to get the most qualified students with the best fit for the organization:

> What often happens is that the service learning program asks me to write up a brief description of what I want the students to do. In some cases the students get to select out of a list, so they might have ten organizations apply but only five of them get selected because that is what the students are interested in. In some cases, it's basically "this is what the students do" and that is it.

Preferred Service Learner Characteristics

What are community organization staff looking for in service learners? Many do not have clear criteria, but others make important distinctions between categories of students, differentiating first between undergraduate and graduate students, and then making finer-grade distinctions that produce a composite definition of the ideal service learner.

Service learning students include both undergraduate and graduate-level students in a variety of disciplines. Of the sixty-seven research participants interviewed, twenty-six reported that they had worked only with undergraduate students, thirty-three worked with both levels, and eight did not specify. Organization staff saw challenges in working with undergraduates that related to their level of maturity, their level of professionalism, and their work quality.

Despite those misgivings, there were things that organizations liked about undergraduates. Nine organizations had primarily positive commentary on working with undergraduate service learning students, and saw the final outcome as positive, even with the challenges. Evidently, undergraduates are in plentiful and ready supply, and in some situations (like working with middle school or high school youth), they are seen as "more hip" by the younger kids and have an advantage over older adults in building rapport. They can also have an almost endless supply of energy and enthusiasm, which is invaluable in situations like after-school recreation programs:

> The [undergraduate] college student has really been our key solution. I can't see that changing, despite schedules and short time commitments. . . . I think that's why the college students are such a good fit for our program; they can relate better, they can establish a relationship in trust faster.

With that youthful energy, however, often comes a lack of maturity. Six organizations cited immaturity as a significant challenge in working with undergraduate service learners, especially first- and second-year students, as illustrated by these two interviewees:

> Some [service learners] are just more mature, more motivated. The younger the student, the less invested they seem to be.

> It might be a maturity issue that students who have been in college a little while longer see their classes as being more of a job or that they need to be more responsible for them. The only time[s] I've had problems in the past have been with much younger, freshman/sophomore-level students.

Related to the issue of maturity and professionalism is the feeling among some agency staff that undergraduates do not understand their importance to the organization and the obligations that entails. A quarter of our organizations saw undergraduate service learners as lacking an understanding of nonprofit professional culture and their role in such a culture. On the one hand are those students who enter the situation with a charity attitude that undermines the goals of service learning and who don't take the situation seriously enough. The charity philosophy, which reinforces perceptions of students as giving handouts and community members as unworthy and needy, is one of the most widely criticized aspects of contemporary service learning in the literature (Noley, 1977; Kahne and Westheimer, 1996; Bringle and Hatcher, 1996; Brown, 2001; Marullo and Edwards, 2000; Ward and Wolf-Wendel, 2000). One organization staff person expands on those critiques:

> It can be really hard with undergrad interns . . . to give them negative feedback or critical feedback that they need to hear . . . there tends to be such an assumption [from the students] that because they're here at all, they should get all kinds of kudos . . . and the level of maturity, presentation, understanding . . . has just varied widely from individual to individual. . . . You have some folks who spend the whole time talking on their cell phones, or two interns talking to each other, or they want to chat with the staff, which means instead of getting time freed up, you have staff people worried about getting their work done.

This points to a need to train students in professional etiquette specific to the nonprofit world, which we discuss in later chapters.

On the other hand are those students who can only see the work through the eyes of a corporate culture:

> Undergraduates often "try too hard to be professional" in such a way that doesn't quite fit into a more informal nonprofit organizational culture. It's hard for some to figure out how to "fit in," but "they do get more comfortable through the course of the semester."

The quality of actual work produced by undergraduates is also a factor in community organization staff's low opinion of them. Fourteen organizations cited work quality as a major challenge in working with undergraduates, and here again we see the contradiction between the learning goals and community service goals of service learning. Undergraduates act differently based on whether they see themselves as primarily a learner in the setting, or as a volunteer on whom the organization and its clientele are relying:

I think I've had some prejudice against it [service learning] in a certain way that I kind of imagine, I don't know where this came from—maybe it is from hearing stories from other organizations; that you're seeing the result of some work that you know is sloppy, first-year, freshman undergraduate work. I mean not sloppy—maybe it's very good for where they are, but it's not something that is going to be very useful or up to the standard that we would need.

Sometimes the real consequences of what the students are doing for the client is where the disconnect is. They understand that the client probably relies on this, but maybe they don't realize that the client is banking on it, or the client really needs this to happen for x, y, z reasons . . . they . . . just don't have enough experience with some of these things to be able to make the decisions or to do diligent work that needs to be done.

Consequently, many of the organization staff we interviewed prefer to work with graduate students, or at least advanced undergraduates, and this is also a common preference among community organizations elsewhere (Bacon, 2002). But even places without strong graduate programs can design service learning standards around the characteristics of graduate students that community organization staff value—the maturity of the student, regardless of their class standing, and their ability to commit to longer-term placements. The more-experienced and older college student, especially the graduate student, is often regarded as the gold standard, sometimes even seen as substituting for staff:

The grad students are actually working on providing direct services, twelve to fifteen hours a week . . . we do training for a couple months, that gives us four or five extra hours of staff time, of client time, for the next six months, so that's worth the investment . . . and it's promoting our services; we only have one and a half staff members in our Community Education Department . . . and the amount of time that they spend supervising interns is pretty minimal.

Interview participants stated several benefits to working with graduate-level service learning students, which in many cases involved more intensive internships and practicums rather than the more frequent short-term service learning. Community organization staff gave such field-based education programs extremely positive feedback. Since graduate students tend to be coming out of specific programs that require fieldwork and longer terms of service, the experiences on the whole were much more structured, involved more time, and provided more skilled service than many undergraduate service learners are capable of, as these three interviewees describe:

> I've seen it work much better with the grad students, because their practicum supervisors come in for the meetings, and so there's a definite change—you know that person and you have some relationship to the goals of the program.

> Graduate student interns are fantastic and spend a lot of time here . . . they know what we're doing, the profs know what we're doing, the work they contribute is significant.

> Graduate students are more motivated, more focused, [with] more skills. They are building their career, and that works better for us . . . undergraduates on the other hand might lose their interest in our work after a semester. There is no continuity.

Discussing the advantages of graduate-level service learners provides an initial foundation on which to build a definition of the ideal service learner. Again, that definition begins with the issue of maturity. Four organization staff members stated directly that they were looking for students who were self-motivated, who "can move forward and just do it" without "standing around and waiting for specific instructions." Some also prefer active people who get involved, get "down and dirty" in the activities of the organization, and "don't consider anything beneath them." In the same sense, they are looking for students who are outgoing and work well with people, especially when working with populations of different backgrounds than those of the students:

When I think about the number of interns that we've had,
they've been regular students who've come from small towns;
this is a new experience for them. . . . In terms of my experience, [they are] very conscientious, wanting to learn, really
valuing the whole family structure, open and wanting to have
an experience with a diverse population.

They prefer those students who are interested in gaining general
experience in the field, exploring "new passions" and possible career
paths, and developing personal skills. They appreciate those students
who "want to learn about people that are different than them," and
"care about our community."

Organization staff also tend to look for professional and responsible students who—regardless of age, work experience, and busy
schedules—are "able to manage [their] time very well" and be accountable for their actions. One organization director who worked
with two service learning students on the same project provided a very
insightful comparison of the two service learners in relation to these
variables:

One of the downsides of [service learners] is that you never
know going in if this is going to be one of those stellar people
that perform like a staff person and you wish you could hire
them, or if they're going to flake out midway through and not
follow through . . . especially in the context of one semester,
it's really not enough time to figure that out, if that's somebody
who's going to be worth putting time and energy into. . . . One
of [the students] worked on media and outreach and analyzing
our [sexual assault awareness] . . . and was just phenomenal.
[She] put in way more time than required. The other one was
a really good-hearted person that just didn't have the time to
meet the commitment that the program asked, which wasn't
even to go above and beyond like the other person did, so we
had a really mixed experience just in that little microcosm. . . .
They came from the same class; one was a sophomore premed
that was way overwhelmed, the other was a senior communica-
tions/media major, with hardly any classes left to take, and just

really wanted to do this . . . so I think that individual situations make a huge difference.

Actual skills are also an important consideration for organization staff when they think about the ideal service learner. The vast majority of organizations mentioned a preference for service learners with some type of applicable knowledge. As one interviewee explained:

> We have some people that were kind of high maintenance that came in. . . . And then we spend the day, here is the computer . . . and you have got to spend a lot of time getting people oriented to how we do things. People have to come here with a certain level of skill.

While most organizations looked for a certain level of competence and general skills, more than ten had very specific skill requirements, most often knowledge of a foreign language or a certain level of schooling:

> And in any event, we require that anyone who works here has had experiences living in cultures that are predominantly English-speaking and cultures that are predominantly Spanish-speaking, so if it is a European American student, we would require that they had spent at least a semester living and studying abroad or just living abroad in a Spanish-speaking country.

Others have more general expectations. For example, one staff member mentioned that, "Usually, in the department [the students come from] they have completed all their course work and I think that is the key." A few of the organizations require students to have had certain relevant life experiences or a certain level of knowledge of the organization; skills not necessarily learned in a classroom:

> To be helpful for us, you typically have to bring a range of experiences. . . . A lot of it is connected with comfort with working with regular people.

Then there are the organization staff who prefer that a student have certain skills, but are willing to accommodate those who do not by assigning them different tasks:

> Usually I put something in about it being helpful if you speak Spanish or if you want to do these things you need to speak Spanish, so we tend to get people who do at least speak a little, but if they didn't, we can find things, but they're not as . . . [Interviewer: versatile?] Yeah. They can do the food pantry; they can do the ESL course, but not other things like the reception desk.

Professors play into this situation as well. A few of the organizations commented on the role that professors can play in making sure a student is a good fit for a particular organization:

> I think where the intern situation works really well is when you have field instructors or university people who know their students and place their students in appropriate placements.

> I think it is important for faculty members to spend time with the community to see what happens, build relationships, and make a good fit.

One challenge cited by nearly a third of the organizations is that students participated in service learning primarily to fulfill a class requirement, without necessarily caring about the work itself. The problems caused by this credit-driven motive are exacerbated by the fact that much service learning is not only required but short-term, as we explore in Chapter 4, which is a significant problem in itself. Most organizations were frustrated with this attitude, noting that it produced either neutral or negative results for both the student and the organization:

> If they're just doing the twenty hours and they don't really engage themselves in what we're doing, and don't really ask a few questions and don't really get it, then they're not going to take away as much as if they really invest themselves for [a certain amount of time] in what we're doing.

Some organizations echoed the concern expressed by one staff person that "[this] person could just find something else to do because it's a lot of work to make those matches . . . schedules, etcetera."

The Role of Organizations' Expectations in Selecting Service Learners

Whether or not the organization is able to recruit its ideal service learner, the student and organization must find a match of expectations (Jacoby, 1996). It can't be stressed enough that, if this step is overlooked, the service learning arrangement may run into some serious structural difficulties once the student is actually on-site and working. Some organizations do try to match students with their expectations for the work they need done. However, the matching process can be complicated by students seeing themselves first as learners and the organization seeing them first as volunteers. The service learning literature emphasizes the difference between service learning and volunteerism or even campus-based community service. Service learning, the experts say, is based on an explicit and essential linkage of service experience and course content, with each informing the other (Eyler and Giles, 1999; Fiske, 2001). These definitions seem to be based on the pedagogy developed and adhered to at many educational institutions.

Maybe the community agencies didn't get the memo. From the standpoint of the organization staff we interviewed, and as seen in Chapter 2, the distinction between community service and service learning was not prominent. Only eight agency staff commented on whether or not their expectations for service learners differed from what they expected from other volunteers or staff. Five of those organizations mentioned having the same expectations for students as they do for either regular volunteers or employees, and only three made a definite distinction between the students and other groups. In many cases, the staff we interviewed didn't even know if the students at their agency were receiving course credit. So when we asked the organization staff members about how they determine and communicate their expectations for students, most of them approached the question from the same framework through which they develop expectations for volunteers, and a few apply the same standards as for their staff:

I often do an initial conversation with these folks to say, "I treat our interns like staff; essentially, we have the same expectations that they're going to be here, and if they're not, they let us know." I'm sort of the bad cop, and then their supervisor gets to be the good cop, and that works pretty well [laughing]! Because volunteers that you can't count on, in any capacity, aren't worth having, and we're real clear with people about that going in; it's better than getting midway into it and them ending up getting bad grades from it, and us ending up frustrated with projects undone.

Approximately fifteen organization interviewees mentioned the importance of sharing clear and defined expectations with the students during the recruitment process. If they don't do that, they could be recruiting students that they don't want, as these two staff people illustrate:

I think another thing that is really important in doing this is to have some mutually agreed-upon objectives to this project. If you don't have that, then I don't think anybody is going to be satisfied.

I think agencies have to be honest with the students too, you know. You can't just sort of sell this in a way that, you know, you have got to talk about the glamorous things you do, but, you know, on Wednesdays you take the trash down to the curb, Fridays you water plants.

Another aspect of this issue of expectations is the question of *whose* expectations should be a priority in the service learning relationship. Historically, service learning has been structured to meet higher education curricular objectives (Boyer, 1996; Bringle and Hatcher, 2002). Here the service learning dialectic becomes prominent, as the focus on institutional needs can actually undermine community needs. This dialectic has created problems throughout service learning's history for community organizations, as seen in Chapter 2. And it is not as easy as the analysts imply to find a good match between community and student expectations.

Another way that the dialectic exerts itself occurs when the higher education bias of service learning pressures the organizations to support student-defined projects. Five organization interviewees specifically mentioned situations where the outcomes of student-defined projects created problems:

> We sort of learned our lesson a couple of years ago. A lot of it comes down to making sure the student is a good fit because we have had a couple of situations where someone came to us saying, "I want to do this." When someone comes to you like that, your gut reaction is, "Well, this is great; we'll find something for you to do." But I really think you have to interview them because we have ended up with a couple of people who came to us saying [that] and then we have realized very quickly that they actually were not a really good fit with what we wanted them to do. I don't think they got much out of it and we didn't either. It ended up just sucking our time rather than helping to build on what we are doing.

One staff member articulated particularly well how they needed to protect their own organization's interests in the service learning relationship:

> They came in with really sort of clear learning objectives . . . there was some negotiation at the beginning of that process about what would fit . . . so they get a general sense of the agency's stuff, but the learning comes from the processing they do back in their class and the journals they write and analysis that they do; and from our perspective, that works a lot better than coming in with really rigid goals to do like, these four things while they're here, but these may not be things that we need done . . . so how much are we getting out of the experience, and how much are we accommodating some sort of preformed expectation? We're not an educational agency, so the main point for us is—we're glad that they're learning, but we're really focused on the service that we're getting from them, so if it's more about them, then it's not worth it for us to do it because it ends up diverting energy away from our mission.

Conclusion

We have documented a variety of ways that community organizations find and choose service learners from colleges and universities. The type of student—his or her interests, skills, background of course work, and major—all play into the fit that a particular student will have with an agency. It is really crucial to communicate the expectations on both sides, as we again address in Chapter 6. Aside from these individual characteristics factoring into the success of a project, however, are the ways that the service learning has been structured by the institution. As we have alluded to in this chapter, underlying the issue of finding the right students for a certain organization's needs are problems created by the institution's focus on structuring service learning as primarily a short-term learning experience for students, rather than a long-term commitment to the community. The short-term service learning model is so great a problem that we needed to add a separate chapter of evidence on this phenomenon. It was one of the most provocative findings of this research, as we didn't go into the interviews expecting this to come up, and most of the current literature did not alert us to be on the lookout for it.

4 The Challenge of Short-Term Service Learning

AMY MARTIN, KRISTY SEBLONKA, AND
ELIZABETH TRYON

Introduction

Perhaps one of the most popular forms of service learning today is the service learning component grafted onto a regular course, which nearly always involves a short time commitment on the part of the student. In this study, one of the most consistent themes involved the challenges associated with short-term service learning, which is somewhat surprising given how seldom the problem of "time" has been raised in the literature (see Wallace, 2000; Daynes and Longo, 2004; and Birdsall, 2005).

Loosely, short-term service learning would be described as serving a few hours at a time over the course of several days, or an hour or so a week during part of a semester. But even service learning experiences lasting as long as a full semester are considered short-term by many of our community organizations. In our research, twenty-one participants

---

An earlier version of this chapter appeared in Elizabeth Tryon et al. 2008. The Challenge of Short-Term Service Learning. *Michigan Journal of Community Service Learning* 14 (2): 16–26.

reported working only with short-term service learning students, and the rest had worked with students for both short-term and longer periods.

Small- and medium-sized community organizations—those that have the most to gain from quality service learning and the fewest resources to waste on ineffective service learning—often find short-term service learning to be an unhelpful time sink. The challenges of short-term service learning fall into the following categories:

- *Investment of Time in Working with Short-Term Service Learning Students:* The amount of service provided by students may not produce enough benefits for either the student or the community to justify the effort, particularly since short-term service learning seems to generate less commitment on the part of the student.
- *Incompatibility of Short-Term Service Learning with Direct Service:* Organizations that provide direct services where trust relationships with clients are important find short-term service learning to be especially problematic, as students leave just when trust has been established.
- *Issues with Timing and Project Management:* Short-term service learning makes it difficult to fully develop projects and carefully reflect on them.
- *Community and Campus Calendar Issues:* The academic year issues that make all service learning difficult create even more problems for short-term service learning by reducing available hours and consistency.

Investment of Time in Working with Short-Term Service Learning Students

A lot of short-term service learning is done as a class requirement, often with little consideration of its impact on communities (see, for example, Reed et al., 2005; Fitch, 2005), creating a dual sense of frustration for the community organization. First, the experience is often too brief to greatly benefit either the organization's mission or the student's learning objectives. Second, the often mandatory nature of such short-term service learning requires the organization to deal with the potential for student resentment and less-than-quality performance.

Nine organizations said they were hesitant to invest time in service learners who treated their service experience as a class requirement or obligation, and thus lacked altruistic dedication and commitment, as these two staff members observe:

> They [students] tell us right out that "it seemed better than writing a paper." We know automatically their hearts weren't invested. More-invested students say things like they like working with children, or have experience working with children.

> I think the biggest thing is that students are not willing to go above and beyond what their professor is requiring of them. "I am too busy; I have to do thirty hours; that is all I'm going to do. I can't do six months."

Even when the students are thrilled to be there, the simple fact is that these brief service learning relationships are sometimes a poor time investment for the agency. Many nonprofit organizations are operating within tight or precarious budgets and can't afford to spend a lot of time and energy planning and implementing service learning projects that don't give them a good return.

> [Service learning] projects are a one-time deal; next semester, the focus shifts or priorities change. It would be nice to have some more ongoing relationships we can massage and nurture over time. I certainly think you would get stronger projects on both sides that way.

> The whole thing [service learning] takes time and investment in that person, and if we know they are going to go away in a semester, then frankly it might not be worth our time if we are super busy, which we often are.

Many cash-strapped small- and medium-size nonprofit organizations need to rely at least somewhat on skilled volunteers. Consequently, they must invest a lot of time and energy into training and preparing those volunteers. With short-term service learners, it is not efficient to spend twenty hours training someone but then only get fifteen hours of service from them. Twelve organization interviewees commented that short-term service made it difficult, and often costly, to invest staff time in the service learner:

[The intern] is here twenty hours a week. I have a service learner here for just a few hours a week; it doesn't make up for the administrative costs.

Our number-one reason [for not having service learners] is time . . . there are time constraints on both mine and the person who would be in charge of supervising [a service learner] . . . I wouldn't even say it is because they are a volunteer as opposed to a paid staff, it is just the time of having to supervise somebody else in addition to taking on all of your own responsibilities.

In many cases, it is simply not time-efficient for the organization staff to provide the same formal training and oversight to short-term service learners that it gives to people who make a longer commitment:

We really don't have many opportunities for people to come in for ten hours, especially if they're going to be working with children. By the time we are done training them, our staff could have done the same thing, but better.

Also, many organizations do not have the capacity to provide the unpaid education that students and professor hope for, and they must rely on the student to observe and learn on his or her own initiative. One semester is often simply inadequate time for the student to grasp the complexities of the program well enough to do this:

We are always looking for interns, but projects that we tend to have—some of them have a steep learning curve, so that by the time we get someone up to speed, it's really not worth it for one semester.

The lack of commitment exhibited by short-term service learners sometimes can even lead them to exploit the goodwill of community organizations. They commit to working longer than their course requirement in order to get the training, but then don't follow through on that promise after they've met their minimum hours. Eleven interviewees expressed frustration at training students who do not follow through on the originally agreed-upon time commitment. This is a case of the dialectic of service learning, as an organization can lose interest in hosting service learners after getting burned a few times:

> We were getting a fair number of people who said they would do the whole year, so they would do the twenty-five-hour training, and do one or two shifts, and then we'd sign their little form saying they'd got their forty hours in, and then we'd never see them again. That got really frustrating. . . . Often the amount of time—either for the semester or per week—it just isn't really meaningful for what we're doing.

Some organizations hold out hope, however, that the student's initial investment for a course requirement may turn into something more. And it does happen, of course, that students "catch fire" with the mission of an organization or bond with clients, particularly when they are tutoring or mentoring youth, for instance. That possibility is sometimes worth the investment in a short-term service learner. Other times, it's not worth the risk, as these two agency staff poignantly describe:

> Some [service learners] continue on past the semester . . . but that's usually our only hesitation with the [university students] is that time frame, especially if [the children] get real attached to one of our volunteers; the one-semester-based time frame is hard on the kids.

> Part of what we try to do, or hope, is that people will be so into what they're doing that they'll do it on their own then afterwards . . . but when you get certain people who are only doing it for requirements, that can be a real pain, and even less than worthwhile.

Incompatibility of Short-Term Service Learning with Direct Service

Fourteen of the people we interviewed agreed that short-term service is often a particularly bad fit or inappropriate for direct service, especially when working with youth. Noley noted in 1977 that "CBOs [community-based organizations] believe students spend too little time actually working to make meaningful differences in the lives of clients served at their site." But the actual situation may be even worse than just not meaningful—it can do harm. Oftentimes, programs for young people are aimed at correcting problems associated with lack of good role models and other inconsistencies in their lives. The transient nature of short-term service learners, added to their potential for un-reliability and lack of commitment, only exacerbates those problems. These challenges can be even more serious when the higher education institution and the service learning site are far from each other, leaving underserved rural areas even more neglected when the service learning requirement ends.

Interviewees whose organizations work with children who are homeless or from low-income backgrounds expressed concerns about the emotional distress sometimes inflicted by short-term service learning:

> We do not want to have students come in, meet with them [the children] for a few weeks, then start to get connected and have them drop off the face of the planet. That is not healthy for these kids. They really need to have strong role models in their lives. We ask students to give at least a six-month commitment. But some people would say okay, and then not show up again after they did the commitment they needed to for class.

> For us, a lot of our kids come for three months and then they are gone, so sometimes [short-term service learning] fits. With a lot of homeless kids [however], counting on certain people is really important. If they know that so-and-so is coming back next week, that means a lot to the kids. They have a lot of people that wander into their life for a day and then are gone and they have to start over.

While we don't have the testimony of the children themselves on this matter, it is interesting to consider what they might say if they had the opportunity to compare experiences with short-term and long-term service learners. But as far as we know, there are no studies of client experiences with short-term service learning.

In addition to being concerned about the effect that short-term service learning has on children, organization staff members have learned to be skeptical that college students will continue after their course requirement is complete. Sometimes, as mentioned above, this is because the students are only exploiting the situation to meet the minimum hours stipulated by their professor. But even the students who make a sincere commitment can find their lives changing from semester to semester in ways they didn't expect:

> For the most part, when their semester is up, they don't continue. A lot want to, but because of their schedule changes, transportation issues, or whatever reason, it's pretty rare that we see them again, but we do have exceptions. Sometimes kids will say, "Where's so-and-so?" after a few months of depending on them for homework help or they knew they had someone to play checkers with . . . generally it's too short.

Organization staff, of course, have to focus their greatest concern on the people they serve, and that is the source of their first hesitation with hosting most service learners. But they also question whether short-term service learners can actually derive much deep learning from such limited contact:

> The limited-term aspect is what makes it [service learning] not work for the child-care program; we would like people that can make a long-term commitment. For direct service, I do ten hours of training and a background check, and by the time that process is done, usually about half those hours have already been used. Even thirty hours . . . they come in and do five or six shifts . . . I don't know that it's beneficial for the students either; it's such a limited contact with the program, and it's hard to know where there's growth and learning.

Issues with Timing and Project Management

Nearly one-third of the organizations noted the difficulty of designing a meaningful service learning project to fit a semester or shorter period. These challenges include having ample time to prepare for working with students, delegating work to them, and finding time to reflect with students and evaluate their projects. A fairly common complaint among the agency staff is that it's unrealistic to expect students to prepare, carry out, and reflect on a project all within a one-semester time frame:

> I think it has been challenging the few times we have tried to use [short-term service learning] to figure out the timing of it. Students have a really narrow window at the beginning of the semester where they have to figure out what they are doing and then it is kind of a narrow couple-of-month's window to do it and then they are gone. And it has been hard for us to kind of be prepared enough and have any kind of plan ahead of time on how we might use somebody that shows up on our doorstep saying they want a project.

The interviewee above also mentioned that it is often difficult to manage delegation of work even among organization staff, let alone among service learners who are "short-term and unexpected." Other staff also expressed doubt in their ability to provide the needed support for short-term service learners, noting that their own stressful jobs prevented the depth of planning and thought they would have liked to put into projects with students, and that capacity issues could not be managed due to staff being stretched too thin. Organization staff would really appreciate a heightened level of support from an institutional staff member, someone at a service learning office, or perhaps a temporary grant-funded position or student scholar who would have the responsibility to see the project through:

> For all of the service learning projects we could offer for people to do, there is all of this behind-the-scenes planning that needs to happen in order to get people in a room to do something, so it would be nice if we had somebody who would be able to coordinate that stuff because I just don't have time.

It is, of course, possible for short-term service learning to work, and many times organizations are satisfied with the outcomes. But on the whole, it seems that the service learning projects that are more successful happen when there is a clear, realistic goal between the higher education institution, the student, and the site supervisor—or as one organization put it, a "shared possible goal." Along the same lines, another organization noted that both parties' satisfaction is contingent upon "mutually agreed-upon objectives." The lack of time in short-term service learning to clarify the goal and how it is to be carried out may hamper the ability of all parties to adjust or "tweak" the project as it proceeds, as these two service providers describe:

> The big thing with [this particular class] was, I guess, it was a big misunderstanding on our part, or their part, or probably both . . . what they were doing for us was creating some marketing materials and enhancing our Web site and stuff, and they saw it as a semester-long project, so the product that they were giving us, they looked at as their final. Whereas it should have been done two months earlier because there is a lot of going back and forth with "I don't like this or that," . . . in the real world, it doesn't work that way. You don't turn in a final project and say, "Here you go, goodbye."

> Once the semester is over . . . poof . . . they are gone. Sometimes the works are unfinished, sometimes they are not very good, and they left us a mess. I am very hesitant to go back to [this particular class].

Community and Campus Calendar Issues

There is certainly recognition that campus and community calendars don't correspond very well (Wallace, 2000; Daynes and Longo, 2004). This is actually a problem with all service learners, including even those who commit beyond a semester. What we have not recognized is that the incompatibility of the two calendars can create serious problems in a short-term service learning context. The best advice the handbooks can offer is for community organizations not to expect too much from students between November and January (Scheibel, Bowley, and Jones, 2005). In fact, service learning proponents seem more concerned with protecting the students' schedules than meeting the community's needs (see, for example, Sigmon, Hemesath, and Witte, 1996). McCarthy (1996: 118) also encourages community organizations to be in tune with and respond to the student's time needs rather than their own: "Sites and activities selected should also reflect students' busy schedules. Regardless of the nature of students' motivation to serve, event organizers and community agencies need to understand that participating in service is only one of many demands on students' lives as they juggle schedules that may include working, studying and going to classes; commuting; socializing and attending to family, friends, and personal priorities." This advice is seriously tilted toward the student's perspective, without consideration of what havoc is created by gaps in service when the community is counting on it.

Of those community organization staff who discussed having issues with their service learning students due to conflicting campus-community schedules, some could not see accommodating themselves to the campus calendar without undermining their own mission:

> You lose 'em [undergraduate service learners] for a week over Thanksgiving, and then you lose 'em over Christmas, and then . . . they don't come back until the end of January, and then you've got spring break, and they've got finals . . . and you know, none of those things are part of our calendar . . . versus most of our grad students understand that you can only be gone for a week, because if they've got a client, you can't blow them off for two or three weeks, because if they didn't need to meet with you, they wouldn't BE here . . . but also, we can't afford to put things on hold for six to seven weeks out of the year, because the work still goes on.

Midterms, finals, school breaks and lack of continuity in the academic workload also present challenges for consistency in short-term service learning projects.

> A semester is pretty short, and the problem with the semester is there's a bunch of holes . . . service learning doesn't mean the rest of their classes stop, so they have a lot of demands on their time. And sometimes those demands get way higher, like midterms, finals, spring break. . . . So all those things make it tough to get in and get a unit of work done.

Breaks in the academic calendar create the seeming necessity for short-term service learning, but place real burdens on the organizations.

Agencies have to find ways to fill in during those times when students are not technically in session and don't feel any obligation to work at their service learning site. At institutions where few of the students are local, even the students who volunteer for no course credit are not available during the breaks:

> It has typically been certain times when you don't have enough volunteers. . . . There is also the seasonal issue of people going on winter break. That has been a big issue for us, as much as we rely on service learners. Winter break is a huge issue, spring break is a smaller one, and summer can require a whole new round of recruiting people to volunteer.

As the above quote suggests, the nature of short-term service learning exacerbates this problem. If a class does not consistently send approximately the same number of service learners each semester, there will be gaping holes in the volunteer pool of the organization. In a small college context, where there are fewer courses and a smaller student pool, finding a course to fill the gap could be even more challenging than at a large institution. Granted, agency volunteer coordinators are constantly having to recruit to fill gaps created by people moving on, but if you're talking about half of a class being assigned to one agency, that can make or break a program:

> One year, we had I think eight or nine people who were all from the same class who came out . . . well, that had a really significant impact on [the agency] in terms of needing volunteers . . . literally half my volunteers on Wednesday . . . and Thursday nights had come from this project. . . . The next year, I don't think anybody mentioned it, so none of the students knew about us and so we went from having nine volunteers [from the college] one semester to zero the next . . . and that's a big fluctuation.

This story reinforces the point that students who can commit to an entire year can cut the organization's volunteer recruitment and orientation burden in half. In addition, institutions should be aware that once they have provided a number of volunteers for a semester, agency staff would really appreciate the faculty to communicate early in the semester whether they plan to offer the same opportunity again the next semester, so that the agency can begin to make other arrangements to recruit volunteers if necessary. While it may not be wise for an agency to depend on receiving volunteers from any one source, it is easy to see how a staff member could be lulled into a false sense of complacency by filling the agency's volunteer quota in one phone call.

How People Make the Best Out of Short-Term Service Learning

Even though nearly all of the twenty-one organizations that had worked only with short-term service learners had less than positive feelings about it, eight of them discussed why they continued working with these service learners regardless of the drawbacks. A surprising number of organizations saw mentoring students as almost an extension of their mission, as we detail in Chapter 2. Playing a part in the education of service learners, even when a short-term placement may not serve the immediate interests of the agency, motivated some agency staff to still want to work with students:

> Oh yeah, [service learning saves us time and money] most of the time. We do weigh it, you know, is it really going to be more of our time? You have to analyze each project, each opportunity, to see if it really is going to beat a cost-benefit ratio kind of thing, but in general, like I said, I have a personal bias to working with students.

Other organizations value the perspective that students can bring. In the daily grind of just getting the work done on a shoestring budget, having fresh energy and new ideas can be energizing for the staff:

> It helps our staff with being able to do a better job. They have a little bit more support and they have somebody to work with. I think it's a good experience for the staff that provides the supervision as well as the other staff, to have new people, new faces; just fresh perspectives on things that the students bring. It helps to motivate sometimes, I think.

As discussed in Chapter 2, a number of organization staff opt for using service learners in specific projects as a way to get the most capacity out of the service learning relationship. Project-based service learning is also effective for maximizing the outcomes of short-term service learning (Draper, 2004; Bradford, 2005; Wayne State College, n.d.). The way to manage short-term service learning, according to McCarthy (1996), is to scale the service learning experience down: "Although the impact of a single project may be small, narrowing the focus . . . to one issue—perhaps preparing Thanksgiving dinners for a few families or cleaning up the graffiti on one city block—enables all participants to see tangible, however limited, benefits to the community or individuals served."

Many organizations have special projects requiring technical capacity that organization staff often lack. Having students with specific skills handle such projects can fill those capacity gaps.

> With [a semester-long service learning class], we were looking at some products that were more technical . . . , and those are things that if you had to pay for them would cost you an arm and a leg. And also the learning curve for us, this is something that we have no idea what to do or how to do it. We look to the students for some guidance, you know, you learn it, tell us; rather than us learning it, because of that kind of time commitment.

One agency delineated a special project that fit well into a semester and avoided the scheduling challenges presented by the agency's normal mode of direct-client crisis service. Second-level priorities that are not critical to the mission, not on a strict deadline, and where failure will not disrupt the organization's daily operations also make good project-based service learning opportunities:

> I see service learning working best with sort of "prepackaged" projects that have very defined parameters—that are meaningful, so it's a worthwhile experience—but not so time-sensitive.

This particular organization worked with two students on a media campaign, including an analysis of media process, which happens annually at this agency during the month of April, "so we really kick into gear in January, and then May is sort of the evaluation time . . . so it works well in a semester." But even within this project, the challenge of short-term service learning was evident. Aside from the simple logistics and the amount of time required, it is hard to gauge, in one semester, the students' motivations and personal time pressures, and therefore difficult to predict the quality of the product. In addition, developing a project can itself be a time sink for an organization if there is not a commitment by the institution to provide students for the project when the organization needs them:

> The timing issue, I just can't say enough about that. It's just too hard to come up with things that can sit around and wait until they [might] meet somebody's service learning goals and yet are something that we need.

Beyond Short-Term Service Learning

Service learning proponents may be convinced that short-term service learning is good for students, and there are models such as project-based service learning that can produce tangible benefits for community organizations. However, from our conversations with organizations, it does not appear to be the optimal model. Along with the findings of our research, one of the few studies on the civic impacts of service learning—in this case with high school students—found that short-term service learning produced less civic knowledge and fewer civic skills than long-term engagement (Billig, Root, and Jesse, 2005). And ours is not the first research to find out how much community organizations dislike the practice. Vernon and Ward (1999), Bushouse (2005), and Sandy and Holland (2006) also encountered community organizations that criticized the short-term time commitment of service learning and wanted more than a semester of service. Wallace (2000) relays a conversation between Myles Horton of the famous Highlander Folk School and Herman Blake of the University of California-Santa Cruz, which points out the gulf between the ideal and the reality:

> He asked Horton . . . if students from Santa Cruz could come and do internships at Highlander. "Yes," Horton replied, "we

will be glad to have them, provided that they stay with us for two years."

There are ways to move service learning to long-term commitments. One option is to integrate service learning assignments into "yearlong" courses, where groundwork and training are completed in the fall and direct service continues throughout the entire year. Another option in cases where students can't make the commitment to a yearlong class is for faculty to form relationships with community agencies and send approximately the same number of students each semester, for a set period, so that the agency can depend on at least a certain number of "warm bodies." And that's not the only benefit—building those relationships between faculty and community allows an easier replication of projects because ground rules have already been established and therefore some of the advance work can be cut down.

The desire for long-term service learners was underlined by nearly one-third of the organizations interviewed. In addition to the benefits of a longer time commitment, these service learners are frequently either upper-level undergraduate or graduate students in an internship or field placement, technical college student interns, work-study students, or committed lower-division undergraduates. One interviewee stated that, in contrast to a negative experience she had with an undergraduate service learning class that was "too unstructured," a relationship had developed with another department that was working well:

> I know exactly what's supposed to happen there. I know what they're supposed to learn while they're here. I know what I can expect from them. It helps that they're here for a full year, so there's a long period of time to develop and get things done . . . it's worth our investment because, you know, we get somebody every October who's brand new, doesn't really know what they're doing, but is here for a long enough time, for enough hours, and enough intensity that they figure it out, and so then we get several months worth of really productive, good work from them, and at the same time they're getting really deep, valuable learning from us.

Conclusion

In working with community organizations, it's important to remember that often they don't feel like they are in a position to press higher education institutions to structure service learning so that it better fits community needs. To the contrary, as we have noted, a number of the organizations expressed fears that if they rejected offers of short-term service learning, they might not be offered any help. But they hold out hope for a better system.

We might begin to shift the paradigm by designing alternative service learning structures. One model comes from the Trent Centre for Community-Based Education and the U-Links Centre for Community-Based Research—partner organizations that work with Trent University in Peterborough, Ontario, Canada. Trent University's curriculum is structured around yearlong courses, and service learning is incorporated into many of those courses as part of the university's institutional structure. The design builds on the European "Science Shop" model, which extends service learning and community-based research models and makes them more community focused and project based. Both community-based research and service learning are organized through a process where community organizations write proposals for projects and the Trent Centre and U-Links then locates students in existing courses to carry out the projects (Hall, 2006).

It may not be practical for all service learning commitments to be a minimum of a full year, given the tight scheduling of other pressing graduation requirements in a busy student's program of study. But if higher education faculty, students, and administrators at least recognize the shortcomings of short-term service learning, they can work to mitigate them with better planning. In those cases, another possibility is to avoid placing students in direct client-service roles or any role that requires extensive training. Engaging those who are at the receiving end of service learning, community members themselves, could also inform us much more deeply of the costs and benefits of short-term service learning. Instead, project-based service learning may better fit short-term time frames. Turning next to the "nuts and bolts" of managing service learners, we see how this short-term issue fits into the complicated big picture of the practice.

5 Managing Service Learners

Training, Supervising, and Evaluating

Jason Gonzalez and Barbara Golden

Perhaps one reason so much service learning defaults to simple short-term opportunities is that, when you really think about it, serious service learning involves enormous complexity and commitment. Service learning extends the classroom into the community, be it local, regional, national, or international. It engages students in activities that address human and community needs, but also attempts to meet the demands of an academic curriculum, as students take scholarly knowledge into the community and bring their experiential learning back into the classroom. This integration of pedagogy with real-world experience provides a unique learning opportunity for students, which can result in positive outcomes in their academic learning and personal development. But the sticky logistics of organizing a project can cause problems for community agencies and indirectly affect student outcomes if they are not hammered out at the beginning of a service learning partnership.

The issues identified by community organizations concerning the management of service learners include:

- *Structuring Service Learning:* Should they be in groups or work solo? Can they work off-site? Should they be paid or unpaid?

- *Preparing to Supervise Service Learners:* How are expectations developed? How are they communicated?
- *Training Service Learners:* Who is responsible for training service learners? What should the training include?
- *Supervision and Evaluation:* Who should take responsibility for supervising and evaluating service learners? What does adequate supervision and evaluation entail?

Structuring Service Learning

We have heard about community organization staff members' preferences for finding, recruiting, and selecting service learners, but all that preparatory work only gets the student to the entry point of the project. Planning is but the recipe and, as they say, the proof is in the pudding. So organizations wind up dealing with a range of service learners who have different learning styles and motivations, and it becomes their job to mold those students into volunteers who provide useful service while also becoming imbued with new ideas and values about the organization's work—a rather tall order, perhaps. Positive outcomes for both service learners and agencies can be either greatly facilitated or hampered, depending on the interaction of the traits of the students with the type of structures and processes set up for training, supervising, and evaluating service learners.

We found substantial variation in community organization structures and processes for managing service learners. Much of that variation revolved around whether students worked as individuals or in groups, whether they performed menial or transformative service, whether they performed their duties on-site or off-site, and whether or not they were paid for their service.

There may also be variation in how they dealt with differences in the area institutions from which service learners came, ranging from a small liberal arts college with only 2,500 students and 120 full-time faculty, to a technical college of about 15,000 students, to a world-class research institution of more than 45,000 students. The agency staff didn't always specify which institution they were dealing with, however, so we don't know how much difference there was in how they dealt with students. We do know, however, that there are many more points of entry at the University of Wisconsin, making the process potentially more complicated. Edgewood College, in contrast, has a single office that is able to maintain close relationships with the service learning faculty and keep track of who went where with a little more certitude.

Groups versus Individuals

The decision of whether students work in groups or alone often does not result from the needs of the service learning site; it can just as easily be the choice of the instructor or the students. Some service learning students volunteer with organizations as individuals, either by getting a referral from their professor or finding an agency through their own initiative. There are times when faculty assign a group, or several students choose to work together. Group projects tend to be comprised of several students from one class, though at times an entire class may participate in a service learning project with a single agency. Nearly all of the organizations that we interviewed had experience with individual service learners, but about a third also reported experiences working with groups of students.

Those who worked with groups of service learners did see some benefits to the group model. Some community organization staff found that service learning groups were good at self-managing, which allowed students to share skills among themselves, and helped students learn how to work collectively:

> For the group projects, the group kind of . . . takes on the internal learning. . . . In the projects where there are groups, then the groups kind of do their own policing. They know what is happening; if they are dividing up tasks to get to some goal and someone is consistently not delivering, then they know that. . . . It also helps the students ramp up their energy for getting themselves to do the work because their peers are on their case if they don't.

It's not the case in all sectors and types of nonprofits, but occasionally group work can provide a comfort level for students in a particularly different cultural setting. Some students worry about saying or doing the wrong thing, feel frightened by unfamiliar surroundings, or even have difficulty understanding the experience of the community they are in. Hopefully, among their own group, they can find those who are better able to translate the communication and interpret the experience to reduce the risk of miscommunication and facilitate the development of productive relationships. Assigning groups of students to one agency can also be useful to provide adequate coverage for the agency's clientele. In one case, an entire class of nursing students worked with a hospice agency to record the life stories of the patients on a one-on-one basis. This meant that every patient who wished to participate in this activity was able to record a legacy for their families, and no patients had to be "left out" for lack of a student to be paired up with (Adrian, 2008). Full coverage is particularly relevant for younger children in mentoring programs. When there are too few students to go around, those children who don't get the extra help with tutoring wonder why someone else was chosen for that special attention. If you have enough students, you can take care of a group's needs.

Some organizations practice group work as their norm, and often do not even provide service learning spots for an individual:

> Classes have worked well, but maybe it is because our work is so group oriented. A group of students have been able to work together on something and benefit from each others' skills and talents. . . . We do not do very much having to do with one person; almost everything is about collective action. . . . Our work is not the work of individuals.

Using service learning groups also can make supervision of the project easier. It's not exactly a "one-size-fits-all" approach, but if you have a class, you can train them together, put them to work, and evaluate them all using the same models and standards.

While there are some benefits to the service learning group model, however, organization staff more often discussed the challenges of working with the group structure, noting that there was often unequal participation by group members and incomplete control over the work process. At least four organizations talked at length about these challenges. They obviously did not have the kind of self-monitoring group described earlier, who kept their peers in line:

> You know, you'll always get a few students in a big group who are excellent and very knowledgeable and who will take the ball and run with it and are willing to invest the time and energy to make it happen. And then there are going to be other people who are just too involved in other stuff.

As students ourselves, it is likely that we all have had experiences as the person feeling the weight of responsibility for getting the job done in a group project, and resenting the lack of commitment from our fellow group members, or feeling relieved that there was someone in our group who was willing to do so much work so we didn't have to. One staff member commented on this unevenness:

> I think with some of these students, you have the group dynamic going on . . . some of those team players just don't come through and finish the effort . . . of that group. So the whole thing of it being a group just multiplies possibly the negative or positive impact times four or five or how many people are there.

A few organization staff mentioned that groups hadn't finished projects. One person felt that a lack of skills could disrupt projects, and that a group provided no assurance of adequate skills for a project:

> So I think . . . it was just the group dynamic . . . everyone was kind of looking at everyone else like, "Well, I thought you could do this," "No, I thought you could do this," so all of a sudden, it's like nobody can do it.

Service learning groups can also develop an in-group dynamic that makes them difficult to manage. At least six organization staff members felt a lack of control over group-based service learning projects. One factor that may contribute to this feeling, discussed later in this section, is that most groups complete their service learning projects off-site with only occasional meetings with the organizational staff. It makes the project seem unwieldy, as these two agency staff comment:

> We were able to, sort of able to, direct the project [at first], and then all these other groups were taking them and started moving them in a different way. I think if we had been part of that discussion, then it would have moved in the right direction, but it just didn't. Up until then, I think it went really well.

> [I]t was kind of more hands-off. You know, just when it was supposed to happen, it would happen. And I didn't know what was happening internally.

One agency staff person discussed how he front-loads the communication with groups to ensure more organizational control of the project:

> One of the things I try to do—I think I moved towards this as we've become more experienced with service learning—is to provide the students with as much information up front as possible about what the organization is about, what we are trying to get done in the project, and how it relates to the big picture. Because if you leave it open-ended or give the students too much opportunity to take the project and run, they can develop unrealistic expectations.

Communication can become especially problematic when each member of the group is responsible for setting up his or her own project and contacting the organization. They may not mention they are part of a group, and then the agency has to keep starting from scratch until after maybe the third or fourth phone call, when it dawns on them to ask the student, "Are you part of so-and-so's class, too?" This certainly affects the consistency and efficiency of the project as a whole and undermines whatever advantages the group structure may have had. What may work better is to assign one member of the group as the class's contact person with the organization, with the understanding that they are coming back and relaying the information accurately to their classmates. Mars Hill College uses a community-based research service learning model where experienced and seasoned upper-division students organize and supervise service learning groups (Strand et al., 2003). Faculty at two of the area institutions included in this research are also currently experimenting with such a model, but none of the organization staff we interviewed reported experiences with it.

While we have mostly discussed respondents' experiences with groups, it is much more common for community organizations to manage service learners as individuals. The nature of the work in many agencies is a better fit for individuals by the very fact that they don't have the physical space for large groups, have small staff capacity, or have smaller client bases. Overall, organization staff seemed to favor individual service learners over groups, due primarily to the tension in the group dynamics. But organization staff also saw individuals as more likely to provide longer-term and more-intense service learning, more likely to work on-site rather than off-site, and more likely to develop a personal connection with the organization. The rest of this chapter, then, focuses mostly on individual service learners.

On-Site versus Off-Site Service

In general, group projects were often based off-site, while individuals were more likely to conduct their service learning at the agency's headquarters or outposts. This was particularly true for interns or service learners working in direct-service capacities. Some organization staff believed that they could better manage and form relationships with service learners when they were on-site. For some agency staff, the emotional relationship is very important:

> Where we occasionally run into some not-so-satisfactory situations is where the student wants to work from home and then we don't have that . . . it's like an absentee worker. . . . Some of this they may be able to do from home, but I would like most of the work to actually be done in and around the premise . . . I think it's because it is a relationship sort of thing. You actually have to have contact with someone. I think it starts to break down where you have someone doing the work away from [here].

Other agency staff find that having students work on-site helps them to develop a deeper understanding of the organization's work:

> To their defense, they're not with us forty hours a week, where they'd kind of get it a little more . . . there's a thirty-minute or hour meeting every week [or] two weeks, so there's only so much communication time. You know, they're on campus doing their thing, and we're out here doing our thing, and the two aren't connecting. For interns, it works much better because they're on-site most of the time. In that regard, it works much better. They can kind of get what's going on.

Organizations can also have a hard time knowing how the students are doing when they are off-site:

> So it has to come from someplace to say, "Here's how we're going to focus this energy." If it's a project that's been largely done at the agency, then that's easier to keep track of. If it's a project that the students are taking off [on] their own, to their classrooms or wherever, then that's harder because you cannot see if the student is sitting there with a blank expression or unable to focus on the project. There's no feedback if you are not seeing it happen.

Such challenges are exacerbated when the physical distance between the campus and the community organization is greater, making it both more difficult for the student to work on-site and less likely that the organization will be able to attract students if they require them to work on-site.

The lack of regular contact between staff and student can also affect the evaluation process:

> In terms of grading the performance of the students, I just don't feel like I am that connected to the students to know who is doing what, because my interaction with them is meetings here and there and most of the work is being done in between.

For these reasons, many organizations seemed to favor having service learners work on-site, believing it would contribute to a higher-quality experience for both themselves and the students.

Paid versus Unpaid Service Learning

There were some cases where students were paid for their service learning, though such cases normally involved longer-term internship-style experiences rather than the more common short-term service learning model. At least two organization representatives believe that paying students, such as through work-study funding, increases motivation and work ethic:

> Especially with the work-studies, they bring a good work ethic and energy to the job that staff tends to lose. The other day, a work-study student said, "I have to catch my bus in five minutes, is there anything else you need me to do?"

For some community organization staff, there is a difficult-to-control skepticism with students, even interns, who volunteer their time:

> The question in my mind is: How engaged are students as unpaid interns? First of all, how motivated would they be if they were earning some dollars while they are doing it? I don't know how seriously they take their work.

Such skepticism is not universal, however. Two other organization staff members pointed out the benefits of relationships with unpaid service learners or volunteers more generally:

> You can have a strong support system outside of your paid staff because, you know, we're paid staff. But to have people who believe in who you are and want to invest their time free of charge . . . and the only thing they get out of it is some internal feel-good thing, there's no monetary gain; to me, that's the best ally you could possibly have.

> We will end up hiring some students and we struggle with that . . . we also value highly the relationships that form with people we provide services for and people who are unpaid, because it is a different relationship.

It would appear that in general, when structuring service learning opportunities, nonprofit agency staff prefer individuals over groups in most cases and on-site service learners over those working from a remote location. However, we do not have clarity on any differences between paid and unpaid service learning.

Preparing to Supervise Service Learners

We found many variations in how agencies manage service learners. It is a testimony to the dedication and perseverance of the staff we interviewed to hear their stories about the intensive amounts of energy they devote to volunteers who may only have a temporary commitment to their work. They seem to take on some of the preparation that might more logically be done in advance by the institution, but because the institution is not providing that preparation and the organizations need the help, they are willing to fill in the gap.

Some nonprofits are blessed with enough resources to have a specific staff person who recruits, trains, and evaluates students. Out of the sixty-four organizations we interviewed, twenty-nine are fortunate enough to have a staff person devoted to volunteer or service learner management. Others improvise, largely depending upon what types of service learners they are working with, at what point in the school year they find themselves, and from which program or institution the service learners are coming. A common challenge for organizations is that the time constraints and resource shortages that define the nonprofit sector may interfere with their ability to train, supervise, and evaluate volunteers. Staff people in resource-stretched organizations already have many roles to perform, and they hope that students and instructors will be sensitive to the organization's needs:

> I think the students need to realize that the nonprofits are working on limited resources and that it is really better to call ahead and to plan ahead. I know a lot of times at volunteer fairs we at the agencies feel bad, because you might submit an application and it could be a week before you get a call back and we don't want the students to think that we don't value them or that we aren't interested; it is just that a lot of us are wearing so many different hats. Volunteers is one of the things I do, [but I also do] personnel, facility management, fundraising, press, Web site—it goes on and on.

One organization, after concluding that their strategy of assigning service learners to various staff and programs was not meeting their needs, made plans to hire a volunteer coordinator who would manage all of their service learners and other volunteers:

> We are going to have a volunteer coordinator who is more of an HR (human resources) model so that we don't just use volunteers in kids' programs anymore. We're going to use them in our computer lab, at our front desk, in our administrative [program], certainly in our kids' programs, find ways to do a better job of placing students, but also of doing the screenings that are not done.

While there is a lot of advice on how community organizations can communicate their expectations to students (Honnet and Poulsen, 1989; Mihalynuk and Seifer, 2008), doing so remains problematic for many organizations. Many staff recounted situations where a misunderstanding of expectations led to problems. Students often enter into the service learning project with an unrealistic picture of what the work is all about:

> If they [service learners] are coming into a child-care arena, they may not picture that they are going to be sitting in an office.

In some cases, students become disappointed when their expectations of the service experience are not met, especially when they expect to do things for which they are not qualified or trained:

> We certainly have things to do like kitchen help [chuckling]; we need someone to help prepare a meal twice a week. If that is what they want to do, great. But most students are not willing to do that; they want to be in the [therapy] groups. They don't even want to do child care.

The lack of effective communication of expectations, or screening of students to meet those expectations, can lead community organizations to also become frustrated when students do not live up to the staff member's hopes. And organization staff struggle over how to set expectations of young adults with little practical experience who approach the organization as a learning site:

> We are feeling we need to work on where we draw that line of being flexible and open and understanding, but also setting an expectation of follow-through.

> I think sometimes the students are a little overambitious in terms of what they think they can actually accomplish. Sometimes, we are a little overly ambitious in what we think we can put on them, and on what our expectations are, and of what we think they can accomplish in the time that they really have available.

There are sometimes painful consequences when students enter a service learning site thinking only about their own educational objectives, rather than the community organization's expectations:

> I do have some students that will . . . call at 4:00 and [the activities] start at 5:00, and will say, "Oh, I can't come, I have an exam tomorrow." . . . It's not a good reason because they've known about this exam, and now I have to be the one who looks at this child [whom the student was mentoring] and say "I'm sorry, you can't [participate] tonight." . . . I think having that discussion ahead of time really, really helps.

Some organizations address concerns of miscommunicated expectations, and the consequences that can result, by setting out an explicit agreement between the organization, student, and faculty. Some interviewees described using a fairly formal process to communicate and develop agreement on the expectations, whereas others described more informal methods. Formal methods included contracts or orientation programs for students that specified what the student would do, and who would prepare them to do it, while informal methods were often just casual discussions. Six organizations mentioned that they use formal procedures with written agreements detailing the roles and responsibilities of the service learning interaction, such as the one described by this staff person for student interns:

I definitely wrote up a job description saying, "These are the expectations, these are the duties you are going to have, these are the hours that you are going to need to put in to fulfill this job description." And so I didn't have anything in a formal contract that they had to sign, but it was like, "If you want to do this, this is what's expected of you." So there was a clear expectation of what they were going to be doing and what skills we were looking for. With both of them, even though they had found me, I still did an interview process to make sure that I felt it would be a good fit, that they would be people that would be able to fulfill what I need them to do with the internships, so that was important.

The above quote also illustrates an assessment of "fit" as part of the training that many organizations use. Some supervisors look for that fit in terms of personality, while others focus on past experience:

I interview them. . . . Part of the orientation is they fill out a form that lists their experiences, whether they are paid or non-paid, and that kind of helps me to place them where I think they will work out the best.

Training Service Learners

The community organizations varied in what kind of training they expected service learners to receive prior to starting their assigned duties. More than two-thirds provide some kind of direct training for service learners to prepare them for the specific tasks they will be assigned, though the form and duration of the training varies significantly. But they definitely prefer students who arrive with skills and an ability to relate to people from different backgrounds, to which they can then add specific training:

I felt that [the two interns] both came to the organization with good skills and a good sense of how to interact with our population. So some of the things, just personality-wise, that they needed in terms of interacting with our clients and such, they had—which was good. I still had them both attend an orientation just to get a better sense of our organizational history and what we were trying to achieve and that kind of thing, and both of them felt that was beneficial to them. They had a little bit of training that they had to do because part of the internship involved direct service with being involved with our program, which I felt was important to really get a sense of who our clients were and what their needs were and that kind of thing. But that was only a part of what I had them do; I would also have them involved in other aspects of the organization.

In-depth training is especially important for agencies that deal with direct client service and sensitive issues like rape crisis centers and domestic abuse shelters. Respondents felt that students need to be aware that before they will have the privilege of any contact with clients, they must be willing to complete the training necessary to handle these delicate issues without making matters worse:

The first two weeks is all training. She was inundated with training. And after that, she went and observed.

On the other end of the spectrum are those organizations that provide little to no training, which described the other twenty of the sixty-four organizations. Some organizations have volunteer jobs that don't require any specific training, and sometimes there just isn't the staff capacity, so it limits the type of work the student can do:

Most service learners are not trained at all. Some have some previous experience before but do not have technical club training. We don't give the service learners the hard jobs that the staff do. They are assisting the staff, not directly doing it.

Training doesn't just consist of learning the daily work of an organization. Many students need basic preparation in professional etiquette to function as unpaid staff at an agency. Many times it is frustrating for community organization staff to accept a student into their environment who may know nothing about how to "be in an office" at all, let alone work effectively in the context of their particular nonprofit's culture. As discussed in Chapter 3, students have been known to chat up the staff, talk on their cell phones, dress inappropriately, and generally act unprofessionally, all of which make it harder for the regular staff to get things done. Consequently, this makes service learning counterproductive to the organization that has graciously agreed to take on a student.

Another training need, which goes beyond preparation for the actual tasks that the service learner will be asked to do, is that of understanding and working with difference. The entirety of Chapter 7 is devoted to this issue, but it is also important to briefly address it here in the context of training. The majority of the community organization staff we interviewed reported that they serve a low-income clientele or people of color, but that the most typical service learning student is a traditional-aged, white, middle- or upper-class female, so there is a demographic disconnect between the service learners and the clientele. And while we don't know how important these differences are to the community clientele, we are concerned that students are too often inserted into agencies through the problematic charity service model we discuss in Chapter 3, giving the impression to the clientele of an agency that the students are only "doing for, not doing with" (Ward and Wolf-Wendel, 2000). Some agencies, in fact, would rather recruit their own clients for agency work than to struggle with the difficult acculturation of service learners (Noley, 1977). Service learning has been wrestling with the inexperience and sometimes problematic attitudes of students (Noley, 1977; Peacock, Bradley, and Shenk, 2001; Bringle and Hatcher, 1996), but apparently without much success from the reports of our interviewees.

The training required to overcome the biases of the charity model and to work effectively with difference is beyond the capacity of most small- to medium-size nonprofits. In some cases, it is not even part of their own strategic thinking. One organization representative expressed a desire for the students to come prepared by the academic institution with some of the training needed in the area of diversity. When asked if he thought the race of the service learner made a difference in the success of the placement, he replied, "I think it does. This is a high-minority neighborhood." However, this agency provides no such training for volunteers beyond an informal discussion with the staff member. He also says that he knows it is something he could do more of and suspects that at least some students receive additional diversity training, but he was unsure if the area's higher education institutions provide training. When asked whether cultural-competency training is provided for service learners, another organization staff member responded by saying:

> We say that we aren't able to do it, but we want all of our volunteers to go through some sort of cultural-competency training, because our volunteers are very different from the people we serve sometimes, as far as background and race. . . . We have started it, but it would be great to have that kind of backup from the service learning instructor.

The interview participant went on to say that their organization provides information to volunteers about the training, but it is not mandatory. As of now, very few of the organization staff interviewed offer any form of diversity training, and we are aware of only one organization that requires it.

Supervising and Evaluating

Once a service learner has completed any required training, the next set of challenges comes into play with ongoing supervision and evaluation of the service learner, which varies tremendously from agency to agency. The twenty-nine organizations that had a volunteer coordinator used that position as the frontline supervisor for service learners:

> Being that I am the director of volunteer services, I usually am the main contact that the person would have in terms of becoming involved with our program and then I usually oversee at least part, if not all, of the experience that the person would have. And then just being the liaison between the [service learning student] and their professor . . . I'm basically considered the supervisor of that person.

In the other organizations, service learners are supervised by whoever is available on the staff from day to day, or one person who has the job added on to their regular duties. This arrangement works satisfactorily in some cases. If there is no clear agreed-upon structure for managing service learners, however, or the assigned staff person doesn't have the skill or the time to supervise students, the organization risks becoming less productive. Communication can falter between the student and staff, and among the staff. Important tasks may be done poorly or fall through the cracks. Neither students nor faculty often appreciate how difficult it can be having extra "help" thrust upon organization staff, who often take this responsibility without complaint, even when supervision can take time and energy that is needed for crucial agency activities.

Flexibility seems key to success in the looser arrangements. One interviewee indicated that service learners evolve from shadowing staff to working more on their own:

> We have them do a lot of shadowing in the beginning, but I also approach students from a "What do you want to get out of this internship and how can we do that?" and put the responsibility on them to think about that. But as the semester goes on, they grow into more independence.

The director of one agency employs an informal style of what he refers to as "checking in" with his volunteers. He says:

> On a very regular basis, we [director and practicum students] have usually very short conversations: checking in, how are things going, are things the way you expected them to be, you know, what could we do to make the experience better for you, did you feel like you had everything you needed to facilitate activities?

If supervising is sometimes dicey, evaluation can be even trickier. Since service learning courses are not traditional learning experiences, this can leave the community organization, the service learner, and the faculty uncertain as to what might be the most fair and effective way to evaluate the student academically (Peacock, Bradley, and Shenk, 2001). Sometimes the organization staff have no involvement in grading the student; other times they have complete responsibility.

When organizations are involved in evaluating students, it is often in the context of a longer-term, more intensive service learning experience, such as internships. Some staff are left to their own devices to determine the evaluation criteria. Agencies that have regular contact with an instructor or who assist with grading a student are in the minority. Likewise, most organizations had little involvement with grading:

> Not so much for me, other than them [the instructors] making, possibly making the initial contact. Sometimes they ask; they will send some type of evaluation form about how did things go to, you know, to evaluate a particular student, but not always. And so I give all of my feedback to . . . active participants.

> When they have internships, then the professor has come in and met with the staff or the supervisor. With most of the service learning projects, there is not a lot of contact with the professor during the time. But the program staff fill out an evaluation at the end. For some of the early years of the elementary education practicum, we actually got feedback from the coordinators at the [institution]; they gave us the feedback from the students. That was great, but that hasn't happened recently.

Fifteen organizations in our study, however, mentioned that they evaluate students in conjunction with the instructor:

> I was involved in the evaluation process. Both of the interns had university supervisors who would come and meet with me and with the student at least once a semester. . . . My first [intern] I had we actually met . . . three times—beginning, midpoint, and end. But with my second [intern] we only met once; but I had a midterm evaluation that I had to fill out and then a final evaluation that I had to fill out. So that way if there were any concerns and such, I could bring them up midway. . . . While I didn't get to give them an actual grade, I still think that they took into account the satisfaction that we had as an agency.

For those who are involved in the evaluation process, there is a question about what they actually evaluate. Roughly half of the organization staff we spoke with said that they evaluated students based on their service performance:

> We'll give what we think a grade should be based on the experiences and the output that we get from the intern. We have not had an experience where we've had to give someone a grade that wasn't conducive to what they thought they should receive.

But it is not always so easy. One agency director noted that there is almost an art to setting up a situation where the service learners understand that the organization will evaluate them not on the level of learning they can show, but on the quality of work they can provide:

> Part of me being the heavy is to set the tone of: "The learning part of this is between you and the university; we're participating in this because we need these resources to do the work that we're doing, there are people counting on us, and if you're letting us down, you're letting them down, and we won't stand for that!"

Within the organization, the emphasis on providing quality service points to the important dialectical tension between academy and community. The academy evaluates students on whether they can show they have learned things they didn't know before. Community organization staff care much more about whether students *already know* what they need in order to provide quality service. From the higher education perspective, community agencies are learning sites. Kraft and Swadener (1994), for example, discuss how useful service learning sites are for helping students develop skills in democratic process and problem solving. From the community perspective, however, service learning sites are work sites, and they need students to arrive with skills in democratic process and problem solving, among others. Community organization staff, however, continually make concessions to serve the demands of the institution rather than to meet their own needs.

This dialectical tension, of course, then complicates the evaluation of service learners. Some organizations found that the evaluation emphasis shifted more toward the student's performance in the service learning placement for more highly skilled students. Thirteen of the interviewed organizations noted differences in expectations for evaluation based on the status of the student. Evaluations of graduate students, field students, and interns were much more structured than they were for undergrads and especially for short-term service learners:

> Field students are a little different than service learning students because they are actually graded on what they do here. I think service learning is a concept that enriches your understanding and gives you practical experience, and field studies are a little more intense. They are graded; you have constant evaluation and feedback. Our volunteers are evaluated every six months or when they want to have promotion. A volunteer might only meet with a staff member when they are with a client, but field students have weekly supervision and feedback.

This staff member also reported being able to influence the grade that the professor gave to the student, which was not always the case by any means. In fact, it is not always clear to organization staff that their evaluation efforts have any effect at all on the student's grade:

> I usually just fill out this evaluation form and then just send it, send it back in. So I don't know how much weight it carries or if it carries any weight at all.

When organization staff go to the time and trouble of completing an evaluation, and then hear nothing back from the faculty member, they worry whether students are being evaluated at all on their performance at the agency. Their concerns are warranted. In the worst-case scenarios, the professor makes no attempt to seek an agency evaluation or to evaluate the students' service learning performance on his or her own. An agency representative relates one such story:

> And I don't know on the professor's part, if there was a lot of follow-through on them, checking up on whether they had

completed it. I was never very clear on that and . . . I just happened to see her at a different event and she said, "Oh, did the students do a good job?" Well, that surprised me because I would think that she would have known if the students had done a good job or not. . . . And I remember her being very surprised when I said, "No, because they didn't finish." . . . So I did think that was funny that she hadn't looked at what they had done to see what they'd completed.

Such ignorance can be interpreted as a real slap in the face, and the usual excuses of being busy and distracted only add insult by implying that the agency's work is not important enough to warrant the professor's attention. We can imagine such disrespect leading community agency personnel to the conclusion that hosting service learners just isn't very practical for them.

One interviewee, while not deterred by the evaluation process herself, spoke of colleagues who saw evaluation as a deterrent to taking on service learners. And even this interview participant referred to the experience of tracking student hours as "very intense." Indeed, if a nonprofit staff member has to spend hours training a service learner, has to track his or her activities, and then has to complete a detailed evaluation form, and only gets twenty hours of service from that student, they are facing a potential net loss of time and productivity.

By and large, service learning may actually place an additional burden upon community organization staff that overshadows actual service learner productivity. At the very least, then, faculty and staff on the institution side can manage the front- and back-end paperwork (such as memoranda of understanding, liability forms, background checks, and so forth) and evaluations in such a way to make the burden as light as possible (Peacock, Bradley, and Shenk, 2001: 31). Some institutions provide handbooks for agencies that delineate tasks to be completed by each partner in the relationship (see, for example, Boise State University, 2005), though it is unclear how widely such documents are distributed and whether there is an accountability process to make sure they are adhered to.

When things aren't spelled out, the relationship surrounding the issues of grading or evaluating can lead to some perhaps problematic and uncomfortable creative adaptations, as the following interviewee illustrated:

> It can be really hard to figure out how to get the feedback directly to the student versus giving it to the professor and influencing their grade. That can be really hard for the staff person doing the supervision. There can be almost a collusion like, "I'm going to sit with you and give you this feedback, but I'm going to give you an A on your grade, because that's the professor, and he's out there somewhere, and you and I are here working together." . . . So I have seen that kind of relationship develop, where the grade is sort of external, and then there's what is really going on, and they don't always match real well.

In the worst cases, the evaluation relationship can become truly dysfunctional. The following quote illustrates how far off the track things can go when appropriate checks and balances have not been put into place:

> We may feel like we owe the student something, because they're here and present and doing something, but if they're often late—you don't want that they get a bad grade—but you want some mechanism to get that feedback to them. . . . Sometimes it's almost like a "Don't make me tell your dad!" kind of thing. "Let's just work this out between ourselves; don't make me have to tell your dad when he gets home!" Affecting their grade becomes a really big hammer, so you don't want to do that, so you end up telling the professor that everything's okay. . . . And then telling the student, "You know those times you were late, we talked about that." . . . There's sort of a disconnect sometimes, because you have a person sitting in front of you that you don't want to mess up their GPA. Or if it's a midterm evaluation, you've got to keep working with them. Or if you get them mad and they leave, you've wasted all that time. It's a weird balance.

We should also consider whether the time community organization staff spend in completing student evaluations for the institution could be better used to evaluate the impact of the students on the community itself. Such evaluation of community impact is a challenge for community organizations overall, and higher education resources that support evaluation of student impact in the community could be combined with efforts to assess overall community impact.

Conclusion

There is much more complexity to managing service learners than just taking a call from a professor who would like to send some students out into the community and the staff person saying, "Okay!" It's imperative for the academic world to honor the tremendous amount of work and responsibility that community organizations put into accommodating service learners, before they stop being so cooperative. Institutions of higher education must become better partners in executing these projects to ensure that they are not only learning opportunities for the students they are charged with teaching, but also that a major lesson the students are learning by example is that the work of the agency and its organizational structure is respected by the academy.

Accomplishing such a mission requires crossing the cultural barriers that divide community from academy. So far, the community has had to accommodate the needs of the institution. We are learning here that, as a consequence, service learning may be detracting from the development of our host communities rather than supporting it. The organizations that faculty send their students to are the intermediary between the community and the academy. But we must deal with the fact that there are profound cultural differences between the academy and the community organization that require very careful attention to communication and relationship building.

6 The Heart of Partnership

Communication and Relationships

ELIZABETH TRYON, AMY HILGENDORF,
AND IAN SCOTT

It's no great surprise that, according to the community organization staff we interviewed, an important factor in the success of service learning is the type of relationship they have with their partner higher education institutions. An important component of this relationship is the nature of the communication between the nonprofit staff and higher education institution representatives, which differs depending on the size and nature of the institution and the structure in place for community engagement.

While this may seem obvious, the staff we interviewed consistently cited problems communicating with faculty and others in the higher education system. In fairness, nonprofits have their own hurdles to overcome. The unpredictable daily overload of nonprofit work can relegate good partner relations to the bottom of the pile until it becomes the crisis of the moment. For example, we know one executive director of a relief agency who often must cancel meetings with partner groups due to emergencies—such as another immigrant family showing up at his door needing immediate assistance.

So what keeps them coming back to the service learning table? It may have something to do with the nature of nonprofit work and the people who commit to it. These are people whose hearts are filled with caring and compassion, and the work offers rewards that are difficult to find outside of the nonprofit sector (Benz, 2005). Nonprofit staff have a sense of urgency to help fill desperate needs, which motivates them to get out of bed in the morning and face yet another day of budget short-falls, grant deadlines, and short staffing. This same urgency is precisely why organization staff are willing to keep taking on student service learners, despite the challenges of this undefined, squishy relationship. Some need help so badly that they are willing to risk being taken advantage of.

The following data, and more importantly the words of the community partners we interviewed, tell the stories of their relationships and communication with higher education institutions. We discuss the data through the following categories:

- *The Need for Positive Relationships and Mutual Understanding:* How important is the relationship in service learning?
- *The Value of Good Communication:* What are the benefits of good communication in a service learning relationship?
- *What Happens When the Communication Breaks Down?* What are the consequences of poor communication?
- *How to Improve Communication:* How do we create more and better communication without overburdening all parties?

The Need for Positive Relationships and Mutual Understanding

Several researchers (Bringle and Hatcher, 2002; Stoecker, 2006; Cut-forth, 1999) have compared campus-community partnerships to romantic interpersonal relationships. It can be helpful to think of the dynamic in that way. No relationship with a high level of commitment is without some discomfort from time to time, as well as the constant need for maintenance (Buhrmester et al., 1988). An enriching, interdependent partnership where higher rewards are attained in both personal and professional relationships requires work, for nothing good comes without effort. In both of these kinds of relationships, communication is crucial to long-term success.

Some partnerships are like a blind date; they are set up by a department or service learning office that might serve as both chaperone and matchmaker. Nineteen of the interviewees described this to be the case with at least some of their service learners. Other organizations connect with service learning resources at social mixers such as volunteer fairs, faculty-community partner roundtables, and other events. Some lucky partners have always been like family friends, and someone along the line has agreed to sign a memorandum of understanding to cement their relationship. Based on interviews with eleven organizations, Bushouse (2005) found that using a memorandum of understanding helped organizations to better understand what they could ask of students and better judge their opportunity costs in taking them on.

Some of these partnerships build from those blind dates or chance encounters. Scheibel, Bowley, and Jones (2005) frame higher education-community relationship development as moving through five levels: (1) limited awareness of each other, (2) limited activities and expectations, (3) structured involvement, (4) joint project development, and (5) collaboration based on risk sharing and management. We saw similar levels of relationships in our research. Of those organization staff who discussed their involvement with higher education institutions, two interviewees reported formalized partnerships with a college or university. Another thirteen reported strong long-term ties to certain departments or faculty.

Regardless of the type of relationship between organization and institution, mutual understanding is the touchstone of the relationship. Twenty-eight interview participants noted the importance of this concept. Many of them suspected that not only may higher education personnel misunderstand community organizations, but the reverse may also be true. Campus-community partnerships are complicated by the disconnect between the academic world's culture, lingo, and time frame, and the community's somewhat faster pace and necessary responsiveness to issues (Bringle and Hatcher 2002; Bender, 1993). At times, they almost seem to be on different planes speaking different languages, and if they aren't conversant in each other's tongue, communication obviously suffers. But well-established relationships between nonprofit and institution staff can overcome these challenges and lead to a higher level of mutual understanding. In order to have this type of relationship, both partners need to discuss the nature of their partnership; they need to talk about how to organize and manage their relationship and to compare their standards for reciprocity. And they need to discuss how to respond to each others' concerns (Gelmon, 2003). This often requires faculty to broaden their definitions of research, teaching, and service, and to push the boundaries of those definitions on their campuses to better fit the needs of nonprofits (Pigza and Troppe, 2003). This allows each side to clarify their general expectations and their roles and responsibilities:

> That ongoing relationship is beneficial . . . it helps [on] my end to know what those students are trying to accomplish, and I think it helps their end . . . the dialogue allows us to improve the process. . . . [We] don't get into a conflicting expectation.

The faculty's understanding of the nonprofit organization and its mission and processes also positively influences the service learning partnership. It helps everyone get to the heart of the program and derive the deepest learning from the experience:

> I think the faculty who understand what type of organization we are and are not is really important.

> Things that make a difference in terms of success are students having a very clear understanding from their instructor, as well as [the organization], about why they are doing this. . . . It is really important for students to understand why they are doing this and whether their work is considered ancillary to the organization or absolutely critical to it.

Of course, a lack of mutual understanding can create problems for the partnership. Such misunderstandings are standard for the grafted-on project discussed in Chapter 4. A hastily or superficially constructed project doesn't always work very well due in part from a lack of commitment to building a solid relationship and discovering through communication what the community organization really needs:

> I think that sometimes, too, there are some professors that don't really understand it very well. They don't really understand the needs of the community, and they think, "I'll just make this

requirement for twenty-five hours of direct service," without understanding how challenging that is for different agencies— that this doesn't work, it's not a good fit.

Campus faculty are the ones who are now being asked to create service learning opportunities, and many times they don't know what's up; they don't know the community. Because that is not what they are rewarded for; they are rewarded for research.

Often, nonprofits are filling professors' needs . . . I never see a [professor] look for what a community needs and then design their class around that. . . . We go through all this trouble to tell them exactly what we need and then [it] doesn't always matter.

The analogy to dating may be appropriate for a professor taking time to understand the nonprofit's needs and meet face-to-face with organization staff in order to get the partnership off on the right foot. One organization staff member expressed this wish:

To have a department or faculty member or team say to us, you know, "If we were going to send you a student for X hours a week for X weeks, what could they do for you?" And we could say, "Here's a project we could have you do," and then people could decide that's a good project . . . that there be some clarity that there's a match that will be helpful to both the student and the agency.

Another interviewee referred specifically to the way graduate internships were structured at their organization. As we have seen, given the longer time span normally involved with internships and the weight accorded to a graduate-level service learning placement, faculty seemed more inclined to invest their time in developing a strong relationship with the community partner. Of course, it would be highly challenging for faculty to spend an equal amount of time on shorter-term undergraduate placements, but organizations expressed a desire for such face time:

I've seen it work much better with the grad students because their practicum supervisors come in for the meetings, and so there's a definite change—you know that person and you have some relationship to the goals of that program. . . . changes the relationship.

In particular, one interviewee lauded a professor for the commitment he demonstrated to the service learning project. It was highly impressive to the organization that this faculty member surpassed anyone else with his investment in the project. A side bonus was that the professor really learned more about the agency and their work, as well as the meaning of the experience to the students:

He himself volunteered as a tutor and so he wanted to be part of that experience with his students and that made the whole difference—him also saying, "I'm going to be part of this."

Ultimately, when a relationship exists between the nonprofit and the institution, it indicates a level of engagement that can be critical to the success of service learning (Jacoby et al., 2003).

There are certainly service learning projects that manage to carry on even where a strong relationship is lacking, but it's clear the community partners favor the idea of putting energy into the partnership and being treated reciprocally, particularly by faculty who exhibit a committed engagement:

We've had better luck . . . where the faculty person is pretty engaged, aware of who we are and who we aren't.

This understanding may involve some engaging between universities and communities. I have seen this willingness of faculty persons to engage the community is crucial in determining the success of the program.

The Value of Good Communication

Communication is paramount in the service learning relationship: It's the *overall* indicator of the health of the relationship and operative functioning of the service learning projects. Communication is what makes it all work. It's the cornerstone upon which the other components rest, from finding a good fit between student and project; to training, managing, and evaluating; striving for cultural competency; and working with faculty and service learning offices in order to fine-tune partnerships so that they are win-win situations for the student, faculty, and community organization. As one staff member stated, "Communication is key!"

Within the service learning literature, however, communication between institution and organization—and particularly between faculty and organization staff—is not treated as key. Communication is often neglected as a topic in a number of influential works focusing on community engagement (see, for example, Cress et al., 2005; Jacoby et al., 2003; Scheibel, Bowley, and Jones, 2005; Sherman and Torbert, 2000; Kaye, 2004). Here again we see the dialectical tension between a focus on the institutional goals of service learning to the possible exclusion of focus on service learning's community impacts.

When we asked interviewees with whom they had the most frequent contact, forty-five said they spoke with faculty or student advisors. Thirty said they talked to department service learning coordinators or institution-wide service learning centers either singly or in addition to faculty or student advisors. Organization staff communicated with higher education partners through a variety of approaches: face-to-face meetings on campus or at the nonprofit site, phone calls, e-mails, letters, contracts, evaluation forms, and databases. In some cases, a chance meeting in the community leads serendipitously to a partnership opportunity. In other instances, students end up being message bearers, passing along business cards to professors or conveying information on their class requirements to the nonprofit organizations. In fact, nineteen of our interviewees had no direct communication with the higher education institution besides the student service learner.

For those agencies that communicate directly with faculty or staff at the local higher education institutions, the amount and timing of contact varies considerably. As one would surmise, most often it occurs at the beginning of the service learning relationship, when students are being recruited and the service learning project is being set up. In addition, nearly two-thirds of the nonprofits report also being in contact with faculty or institution staff during the evaluation phase of the project. Slightly fewer also check in during the service learning experience itself for ongoing management or problem solving.

A number of conditions can further complicate communication between nonprofit and institution partners. One staff member we interviewed works as a linchpin of a large, grant-funded partnership that involves several types of entities throughout the community, with a network of ties to several higher education institutions. This person freely admitted that communication was spotty:

> Not as much planning and interactions with instructors as we would like . . . not a whole lot of time or thought put into it, probably a function of limited time on both sides.

Problems with communication could also be amplified in a large urban institution with thousands of potential service learners and faculty, or exacerbated in small rural college settings that may lack administrative capacity.

Challenges with the service learning project or student are naturally easier to address and resolve when a good relationship—one where mutual trust and respect has been cultivated—exists between the nonprofit and the institution:

> I've supervised students for eight years and so, of course there are problems from time to time, but because there's a structure and relationships, they've all been resolvable. If it's something I can address with the student, that's where I'll start, and if I'm really concerned where there's something unclear, I'll call the professor. It hasn't had to go any further than that, [but] I could call the director if I needed to.

> A student may not be happy with how it's going, but they wouldn't say anything to me, so I probably wouldn't know. It's happened before . . . but because we had these regular meetings, it came out with the professor that things weren't going well. I had no idea, but we were able to make changes that made the student happier and made it a more positive experience. But without that contact, you probably wouldn't get that because the student

wouldn't feel comfortable. A lot of the times when it's not going well, they feel like you're not giving them enough attention, supervision, or direction, and they feel whiny coming to you. . . . But they might feel more comfortable talking to the professor about how it's going.

Nonprofit staff highly value good communication with their higher education partners. Having an established relationship and open, regular communication with the higher education institution helps nonprofits gain clarity about the expectations for the service learning placement and keeps the process running smoothly:

Service learning requires a successful communication triangle. We [the organization] need to know what our needs are and . . . what our limitations are for doing this active teaching and supervision. The students need to know what their realistic time constraints are. And the professor needs to know what the assignment is. And we all need to communicate those things with each other. So if there is a link in that communication that is broken, it [the service learning experience] seems to all fall apart and not be a good experience for all involved. Things that have gone wrong in the past have been a breaking of a link in the communication chain.

The positive [experiences] are typically with professors who I have a longer ongoing relationship with connected with work. . . . We're just much more likely to be in contact and more comfortable checking in with each other. . . . The more familiarity with the contacts, the better.

Relationships where good communication occurs between campus and community may also lead to opportunities for the nonprofit organizations to improve their service learning process, a theme that was raised by ten different interviewees. This can be an unanticipated benefit of encouraging direct communication between faculty and nonprofit staff:

One professor debriefed us last year. There were some kinks in the system and it wasn't going as smoothly as we wanted. So we listened to his concerns and tried to make some changes.

When Communication Is *Not* Ideal

A surprising number of our respondents described a lack of relationship and effective communication with their higher education institutional partners. For nineteen of the nonprofits, students served as the main intermediary between the higher education institution and the agency, bypassing any direct connection between the faculty or service learning office and the community organization. Without a go-to person to contact, communication and relationships were often hindered and difficulties arose:

We have had students who have done that and say, "Oh yeah, yeah, I will do the six months," sign the contract, then their thirty hours are up and [they] ask you to sign a paper and they never show up again. And we have no connection to their professor.

The students have so much anxiety about whether what they're doing is going to fit what their professor or their program wants them to do, and since we're not part of that whole process, we don't know, and there's not a sort of easy mechanism for having that conversation early on. . . . Especially when it's being conveyed by the student going back and forth to the professor and then coming back to us, and only being here twice a week, it can be long and painful and not very clear.

One of the challenges for nonprofit staff is the unpredictability of communication. Community organization staff have experienced wide-ranging variations in their relationships and communication with faculty and institutions:

Communication levels depend on the particular faculty or department. For example, [a particular department] has really good communication with my site. The other faculty [at that

institution] . . . there is no communication . . . only at the beginning when they say they are expecting to have some students come to volunteer and from there, that's it. There is no
follow up, there is no, "How is my student doing? How is their
attendance? Are they okay with the activities?" I'd think, "Oh,
we should have gotten something by now." And then, you know,
I didn't have a sign of life.

Less-positive experiences . . . [have been when] the level of
faculty involvement is next to none, serving as more of a rubber
stamp where the student gets the okay from the faculty person,
but there's really no communication between the organization
and the faculty person.

To be fair, interview participants also described instances where
some of the breakdowns in communication may lie within their own
time constraints. Despite the wishes and best intentions of the community organization staff, there is obviously a gap between the gold
standard and what actually happens during the course of a project:

We've had mixed experience with [communication]. Frequently, it's pretty poor. It tends to be, "Here's the paperwork,
and here's when it's due by," and not a lot of give-and-take. And
even as I'm saying that, I'm realizing that doesn't necessarily
mean that we would have a lot of time for give-and-take [laugh-
ing]. So it's a mixed message for me, too.

Some sources of dissatisfaction or confusion are due to poorly
clarified expectations of roles and responsibilities of the institution or
the organization. When the partners do not engage in meaningful dialogue from the outset of the project, confusion can result:

To be perfectly honest with you, I was never really sure what
we were supposed to provide. I know I asked that question of
the coordinator . . . but when she and I met to review the evaluation of this intern, that was a question I would often raise: "I
don't know what I am supposed to be doing."

I think that lack of communication kind of left us in the dark, as to whether the type of work we were having them do was pertinent to what the professors wanted or needed them to do.

One executive director of an agency that provides direct-client crisis service laughingly suggested that some type of "prepackaged project" could help streamline and simplify the process, leading to more consistent results on both sides of the partnership:

It would almost be better if it was sort of like a Chinese menu: "Pick three things from Column A and one thing from Column B, and there's your meaningful experience!"

How to Improve Relationships and Communication

Our research did not specifically ask organization staff for recommendations on improving communication, but their ideas bubbled up spontaneously in the course of the conversations. Many interview participants willingly, and sometimes emphatically, shared ideas on how to improve the relationships and communication between their organizations and the higher education institutions. Some of these suggestions may require extra work and time, but organization staff also noted a need for balance:

I don't want to make the process a burden. I just want to make sure we both get something out of it.

I don't think [communication] needs to be huge. It's really important and it's lacking, but it could go overboard easily and start putting all these expectations for meetings: it's impossible to go to meetings on campus, it takes half my day, it's impossible to park, and it's hard to leave. And it would be difficult for professors, too; they don't want to travel to all these agencies. A phone call would be sufficient, an e-mail even; a phone call would be better. Just touch base once or twice during the semester, I would say.

In initiating these relationships, interviewees described a desire for more accessible information from the institution, especially in terms of making contacts. This would be the counterpart to the volunteer database where organizations post their needs; instead listing the types of classes that incorporate service learning:

> My suggestion, probably it would be nice if [the higher education institution] has a central clearinghouse where we can search our need for students in particular areas of interest. . . . Sometimes when we need students with certain interests, we don't know where to start. And having the information in a more systematic way will be helpful. It might help students to have more opportunities, too.

It's important to remember that, from the community organization viewpoint, a major university or even a smaller private or community college can still appear to be impenetrable to someone not familiar with that particular system or the workings of the academic machine in general:

> Time, and . . . not knowing the processes that there are to connect . . . because there are so many different departments in the college, as well. It's like calling the State Department of Revenue. If you don't have the right number to begin with, you end up in a number of places.

> I would love to see much more involvement, but we've never been able to quite make that proper contact—find the right person, find the right contact. That's one of the difficulties. If we have a hole and we think that a student might be right for it, there seems to be no place within the system of service learning to plug that into.

A combination of formal and informal communication may help here (Gugerty and Swezey, 1996). Often, organization staff just want to find someone to talk to, or get more detailed written information from the professor to help establish a good relationship:

If someone came for service learning and I got a sheet of paper that said, you know, "This person is interested in doing a service learning project at your site. They would need to spend X hours; these are the kinds of qualities of service that they need; this is what they have to do. Here are the parameters, does this work for you?" That would help, too.

It wouldn't have to be as detailed, but a few goals on paper for them to achieve, that would be helpful.

It is just a matter of knowing where they [service learners] are coming from and what their experience level really is. I suppose if they came with a letter and it was explained that most students in this class are juniors who have this amount of course work under their belt, that would be helpful.

While some organization staff expressed distaste for the administrative procedures of service learning partnerships, others thought that these could be helpful:

[One department] has an interesting setup where you're working with a professor and their student on the project, but then there's also this administrative layer which guides the internship process.

It's been huge for us to have the [service learning professional on-site]—I would say before, I had never really heard much from the campuses themselves.

Approximately one-third of the interview participants also commented on the assistance offered by service learning offices or other administrative support at the higher education institutions. They felt these to be valuable communication tools for service learning to help compensate for the time constraints inherent in running a nonprofit organization. However, some of the organization staff we interviewed were not even aware of certain service learning offices, and were excited to learn about them during the interview process.

One staff member expressed a desire to see the resources from *all* the higher education institutions in our area pooled in one location or database to enable a kind of service learning "one-stop shopping." Another expressed concerns about plans for a new Web site being designed by one institution's service learning center that seemed to go against the "one-stop shop" idea, preferring instead the existing community-wide database that, although not specifically geared toward service learning, at least enabled them to advertise for volunteers of all shapes, stripes, and sizes:

> I really like to have the [volunteer database] where we go to one spot. They were talking about the need for another service learning clearinghouse [website], and I thought, "Are you kidding, one more Web site I have to check and fill in? Please don't just start something new." There are all these places where we have to go to update it every semester, for work study and volunteering. I think [the current Web site system] is good. It seems like students use it.

It was apparent that organization staff members often feel too busy to jump through more hoops than they are currently using to post information or search for volunteers, and would prefer a system with less time spent on posting, browsing, and updating, regardless of the format or institution where the information is housed.

Other interviewees discussed how the depth or richness of their communication with professors and institutional staff can also make a big difference in the relationship. Good communication can show the agency that they are valued enough by the institution for faculty to take time to really nourish the partnership, and it generates goodwill for future projects:

> There are some [faculty] who will really take the initiative to communicate with us regularly. They'll say, "Can I come to a team meeting and talk with your staff?" We had most of [a service learning office] come and debrief with us for this past year, which was really productive, and lots of great ideas were generated for troubleshooting things that hadn't worked so well. And moving forward . . . so everyone . . . will have a better expe-

rience next time around because we took the time to have that
conversation.

Ten interviewees made explicit comments about wanting "more"
communication with faculty and the institutions. This may involve setting regular meetings and conference calls at the outset of the project
to ensure the service learning partnerships are more successful:

Talking on the phone at least once a week and meeting every
two weeks is ideal. And it's funny, because when it strays from
that, that's where the focus on the work suffers on both ends.

Other interviewees felt a need for more face-to-face time with faculty and institutional staff on the organization's home turf. The commitment and respect for the work of the organization that this conveys
would be meaningful to them:

We would like to see more interaction with the faculty so they
understand our organization and come with a project in mind.
Very few faculty members came and visited.

I think if the faculty and the administration of the [institu-
tions] are committed to this, they have to show up . . . and
demonstrate that this is something that they do in their professional lives.

For others, opportunities to visit faculty and students on campus are
also helpful. For example, faculty can encourage community organization staff to give short class presentations. Some organizations won't
have the staff capacity to do this often, and distance can prevent frequent contact in some rural areas, but the ones that do will be able to
present their programs to the students in their own words. Oftentimes,
they will recruit more volunteers when they can directly express their
passion for the work:

We kind of came up with the idea that . . . if they're interested at
all in having them volunteer with [the organization] that somebody from the project would come in and talk about that, so

there'd be expectations. . . . So that everyone would know what the situation was up front and so that we would know what the class was about—why they were doing this—so that hopefully we could do a better job of fulfilling what the students needed.

One morning, I went to four classes he had and presented. It gave us results and we got a lot of students to participate and that's what we are looking for.

With this evidence showing that many community partners appreciate the invitation to visit classes, another vehicle for interaction that may be considered is some variation of the faculty and community roundtable, where community organization representatives are invited to meet faculty and discuss their needs and hopes. This has been used at Marquette University in Milwaukee for a number of years (Timberlake, 2006), and was just instituted by the service learning program at Edgewood College in Madison last fall. Feedback from these events has been extremely positive and they have been very useful as a tool for institutions that want to begin to develop projects with more input from the community.

The most effective path to improving service learning partnerships is to cultivate long-term relationships. Thirteen interviewees discussed the value of having a partnership with a higher education institution that extended beyond the duration of the current service learning project. As illustrated by the following quotes, these interviewees saw the need for developing more of these relationships:

[Service learning] projects are a one-time deal; next semester the focus shifts, our priorities change. It would be nice to have some more ongoing relationships we can massage and nurture over time. I certainly think you would get stronger projects on both sides that way.

What would probably be the best—a lot of things are inevitable—but if the professor can develop a long-term relationship with the program. . . . And it would help the staff think of this as this person being a part of this class, this program with this professor . . . they would understand what the professor's trying to accomplish. And that would probably be beneficial.

Faculty can build such relationships through some simple activities such as reviewing an organization's mission statement or visiting their food pantry, homeless shelter, or other work site. This activity can bring home the meaning of the agency's work to institutional partners and inform their frame of reference whenever they are collaborating with those community organizations.

As the relationship builds, they begin to move toward a marriage of the two partners, which requires a certain amount of commitment, understanding, and of course, communication. These relationships, when allowed to mature over time, can become the most rewarding in the field of campus-community partnerships—a real win-win for both the institution and the community organization. They can be mutually interdependent, giving each other the things they need to flourish and prosper.

In an actual marriage, if things aren't working out, there is often a divorce. Many times in campus-community relationships, the partnership can feel inequitable (Bringle and Hatcher, 2002). There was a smattering of conversation in our interviews that revolved around frustration over missed opportunities or lack of follow-through and partnerships that had been allowed to drift off, but no real messy breakups in the service learning partnerships of the organizations. That may be one way the romantic relationship metaphor doesn't apply. Since these partnerships are not primarily based on emotion, when things end, it's often just by mutual neglect, a shift in an organization's staffing or focus, or the fact that a professor retires or moves on to a different subject matter and their partnership needs change.

Conclusion

One of the most important issues identified by the community organizations in this study is that, for service learning to be successful, finding effective ways to build relationships and communicate with faculty are essential. There was a broad range of opinions expressed about what the community partners desired from their interactions with students, faculty, and service learning professionals at institutions—just as people in different life stages are looking for different things from their interpersonal relationships. Some nonprofits want well-developed, multiyear relationships with faculty, and others simply want streamlined methods of finding students and completing paperwork. Given the diversity of nonprofits in the Madison area, it is no surprise that each organization will have a different set of needs.

Generally, it appears helpful for the nonprofits, considering the inherent constraints on their time and resources, to be able to find efficient processes for communication and relationship building. Databases or written documents that clearly delineate the expectations on both sides of the equation serve to clarify the relationship. Regular phone calls, e-mail, and face-to-face contact can help to maintain mutual understanding. There are numerous resources for faculty and service learning staff in designing written materials for use in recruiting service learners or sites for student projects (Scheibel, Bowley, and Jones, 2005; Campus Compact, 2003). There is also a collection of resources that pertain to campus-community partnerships, including samples of contracts and memoranda of understanding used by several colleges (Stoecker and Tryon, 2008). Getting these into the hands of either faculty or service learning offices, as well as community organization volunteer coordinators or other staff, can be very useful in eliminating some of the frequent pitfalls and answering the frequently asked questions (FAQs) of both entities at the outset of a project.

An argument can certainly be made for the usefulness of service learning offices or centers to help ease the faculty's burden in relationship development. Service learning professionals can act like chaperones in the first dance of a relationship. They come along to make sure that no one is taken advantage of and that details are handled smoothly. If things are working well for both parties, at some point, the chaperones can safely remove themselves. At the other end of the spectrum, if there is not a good match in a fledgling relationship, they can help ease the partners to more fulfilling opportunities. Again, communication helps everyone feel safe and secure, as well as desirable.

But we must be wary of relying too heavily on a central office to handle the management of service learners—it can become an isolated place where faculty can say, "Oh, we don't have to worry about that; the [service learning office] takes care of all the community stuff." Rather than enabling faculty to remain uninvolved, the most effective service learning centers will strive to thread the pieces of engagement throughout the disciplines and schools, so that every department feels a certain amount of responsibility to contribute some of the talent and skill of their students and instructors toward community engagement. Doing so can improve outcomes for both the student and the community.

However, some of the burden must rest with the faculty, who know better than anyone else what it is they want their students to learn from the engaged experience. From the faculty viewpoint, the institutional structure has been set up such that certain activities (publishing, securing grant dollars, and so forth) are rewarded and valued more than others like service work with the community. Maybe the structure needs to be reworked with buy-in from the top administrators in order to continue institutionalizing service learning. If faculty received dedicated release time from their normal teaching load, they could more easily go the extra mile to follow up with community partners and sustain a meaningful relationship. In the meantime, perhaps it will help for faculty to be aware that even in their bustle of committees, classes, papers, and tenure portfolios, academia really has a privileged existence compared to some of the situations faced routinely in nonprofit environments.

When the nonprofit organizations are satisfied with the level of communication, the service learning projects seem to run more smoothly and nonprofits report greater levels of satisfaction. In cases where communication is moderately to severely lacking, it is seen as a problem that needs to be addressed in order for the nonprofit organization to feel more comfortable with service learning students. As with any personal relationship, without good communication to clarify expectations, prevent misunderstandings, and make each of the partners feel valued and respected, it will eventually wither and die on the vine or explode in anger and hurt feelings. It may seem like common sense, but it is an element that too often goes unattended in service learning partnerships. Devoting some time to improving the level of communication between campus and community is crucial to the long-term success of the practice.

7 Service Learning in Context

The Challenge of Diversity

CYNTHIA LIN, CHARITY SCHMIDT,
ELIZABETH TRYON, AND RANDY STOECKER

While previous chapters focus on issues internal to service learning, the question of diversity in service learning requires us, at least momentarily, to consider the broader social context. This dilemma of diversity is part of the fundamental dichotomy of access to higher education (Tierney and Hagedorn, 2002). Historically, that dichotomy has divided those who are privileged by the kind of stable economic and social environment that produces successful academic skills from those who live in the chaos caused by economic uncertainty and its resultant social disruptions. Much of this division, of course, intersects with historical ethnic and racial oppressions, which creates a double burden for college students who are not only from the other side of the tracks but also from the other side of the color line. And even in rural areas that may lack visible racial diversity, there are often intense class-based cultural divides and severe brain drain as students from successful backgrounds leave, while those with fewer options can neither leave nor succeed in local higher education institutions.

The academic success of students from excluded communities is further hampered by the lack of diversity among faculty. More colleges and universities are recognizing this issue and attempting to recruit a more diverse faculty and student body, but with varying degrees of success. In order for written policies that promote campus diversity to carry much weight, they must be implemented upon a supportive foundation. Higher education administrations have to ensure that their infrastructure can meet the needs of all students, for example, by hiring diverse staff, devoting institutional resources to issues of diversity, and creating programs that are attractive to students from different cultural backgrounds. In rural areas, it is often the underresourced, small private college or community college that needs to find new ways to recruit and support such students.

For many higher education institutions suffering from a lack of student growth, diversity may appear to be a way to fill the enrollment needs. But such a superficial motivation may undercut efforts to build a truly respectful diversity on campus. Regional demographics have shifted dramatically since the late 1990s. The high school graduation totals for white students in Madison, Wisconsin, has begun declining, while the number of Latino graduates is climbing rapidly, even while they still show distressingly high dropout rates (United Way's Latino Advisory Delegation, 2006). These figures are mirrored in other areas of the country (ERIC Development Team, 2001). A recent recommendation from California Campus Compact (Vogelgesang, Drummond, and Gilmartin, 2003) draws on such statistics to recommend that colleges and universities take advantage of the "logical" connection between diversity and service learning for fund-raising and public relations advantages. The assumption is that both diversity efforts and service learning focus on disadvantaged minority populations, but in the end, the recommended merger is in danger of exploiting both for the advancement of the institution.

Colleges and universities have to "walk the talk" to support this newly expanding Latino population, as well as the long-excluded African American population, in attending primarily white schools where the academic programs, campus activities, and support systems are geared toward a white middle-class background and experience. It's not enough to give out a few scholarships and put the word "diversity" in the school's mission statement. A report on diversity issued from the University of Michigan is critical of these types of initiatives:

> Campuses have to do more than just give the appearance of valuing diversity by merely trotting out a diversity plan at the

beginning of each year or during accreditation reviews. Such maneuvers, whether performed sincerely or not, produce considerable cynicism across campus. Supporters of diversity will say that nothing is being done while opponents will argue that the lack of progress demonstrates that diversity efforts don't work. (Wade-Golden and Matlock, 2007: 43)

Sustained efforts, including funding and strategies for implementation and assessment, must be integrated throughout the institution to make the campus a comfortable and safe environment.

Added to the problems created by the overall social context is the reality, as we note in Chapter 1, that the dominant service learning model has been organized from the beginning to promote a charity approach where people with more power—who perceive themselves as having more knowledge and skills—"help" people with less power, who they erroneously perceive as possessing less knowledge and fewer skills (Kahne and Westheimer, 1996; Brown, 2001; Marullo and Edwards, 2000; Ward and Wolf-Wendel, 2000). Although meant to empower and enlighten, such a model is just as likely to reinforce students' stereotypes of the less powerful and increase the resentment of those subjected to the help.

Diversity is possibly the thorniest issue facing service learning in higher education today. If the institutional culture and structure is so inadequate for supporting diversity among faculty and students, and the service learning practice is so driven by the charity model, how could it possibly provide effective service learning to diverse communities?

It is very clear how poorly the institutions of higher education reflect and involve their host communities, and particularly those communities with less power. It is also quite clear how broader structures of corporate and government power exclude so many communities from access to resources. But even many of the nonprofit organizations that attempt to redress that inequality are as much a part of the problem as they are a part of the solution. Diversity is a challenge not only with the identity of the service learners but also the staff of the organizations themselves. When we asked nonprofit representatives to describe the demographic characteristics of their staff, service learners, and clients, they recognized many aspects of identity: race and ethnicity, class or socioeconomic status, gender, age, disability (physical and mental), sexual orientation, geographic origin (rural or urban and local, out of state, or even international) language, (non)criminal background, education, religion or spirituality, professional status, and exposure to other cultures and environments. In general, neither service learners nor the organization staff reflect the demographics of the communities they work with. Both service learners and organization staff are predominantly white, middle class, and from dominant mainstream cultures.

We are not in a position to take on all of these concerns; instead, we limit ourselves to the issue of diversity as it relates to service learners themselves. As a whole, our findings highlight a concern that service learners rarely reflect the social demographics of the communities they serve. How do the differences between students and diverse community members manifest themselves in service learning and impact these experiences for the student, the organization, and the communities they are serving? The main themes we address here are:

- *Valuing Diversity:* How important to community organization staff is diversity among service learners?
- *Dilemmas of the Diversity Issue:* How difficult is it to provide service learning that empowers communities when there is so little diversity in service learning?
- *Impacts of Diversity:* What are the positive outcomes of making diversity central to the practice of service learning?
- *Managing a Lack of Diversity:* What do organizations do when they can't access diverse service learners?

We then look at the issues involved in trying to design diversity-training programs that adequately prepare service learning students to effectively work with the communities they are likely to encounter.

Valuing Diversity

Diversity is a crucial element in the missions of many of the agencies themselves. Out of the organizations we interviewed, forty-five representatives described their nonprofits as committed to serving a diversity of groups and creating a vehicle for greater citizen participation in their communities. This sentiment defines the nature of the organizations themselves along with the nature of the service learning experience:

> We believe that by working together we can help our neighbors build community in their neighborhood and improve the spiritual, physical, and mental health of the residents. We also recognize the opportunity to strengthen race, class, and cultural relationships in [our neighborhood].

Exemplifying the value of diversity, one interviewee states: "We believe in the concept that everyone is a learner, a teacher, and a leader."

There is, however, a gap between what organization staff value and what they are able to achieve in the area of diversity with the service learners they have access to. Of the forty participants who discussed the identity of their service learners, two-thirds directly indicated that an overwhelming majority are white and female. Although nonprofit staff express concern that the service learning student population is "not as diverse as we would want it to be," they were often optimistic about the situation and the trend toward representation:

> We would like to see more African Americans, Latinos, and Asians, although this year I've seen more Asian American students come through.

> Most are white women, though this is changing especially with the new Latina sorority on campus.

> I joke with my volunteers, "Suddenly you become the minority in my center." We do have a few Southeast Asian volunteers and a few Latino and African American, but the majority of the volunteers will be women with Caucasian background. Personally, I believe it doesn't make any difference [to the success of the program].

Expanding the diversity of the staff and the service learners is a common goal for community organizations. A number of organization staff, however, present diversity as secondary to the greater mission of the agency:

> We don't really address diversity [in staff], not because we don't want to, but it is just how we have been doing it and it has worked well.

You know, male, female, transgender; young, older, non-traditional—none of those things come into play when we're looking at an internship. We look at, "Here are our goals and objectives, here's the mission of our agency, and how might that fit into the personal mission and the development of this prospective intern?"

Unfortunately, we do not know if the agencies' clientele would agree with these sentiments, but it is worth considering that one of the challenges facing diversity in service learning is bringing community members fully into the service learning design process.

The Dilemmas of Diversity

It is unclear whether the extent to which diversity does not surface as a central issue for more organizations is the result of the difficulty that people with white privilege have recognizing the problems created by a lack of diversity, or because the staff are simply resigned to the lack of diversity in the organization itself and among the service learners they host. Regardless of the cause, the challenge created by the reality of racial and ethnic inequality overall, and the mirroring of that inequality in nonprofit and service learning leadership, is a central aspect of the internal contradictions of the service learning dialectic. A few interview participants voiced the generally held impression that the Madison area is not very diverse, especially in respect to race and ethnicity, while others mentioned that there are few minorities in service-related fields. But we know that a predominance of nonprofit agencies serve a population that consists primarily of minority-identified clients. Political rallies, such as the 2006 "Day of Action" march in support of immigration rights, provide evidence that contradicts the impression of a homogenous city. Recent research also supports the notion that the region is becoming more diverse (United Way's Latino Advisory Delegation, 2006). However, as has been noted, that diversity is not well represented among either the higher education institutions or the nonprofits. Clearly, this issue presents a dilemma for local nonprofits in their mission to value diversity.

The reality that service learners often come from a privileged race and class background, compared to clients of many agencies, provides a challenge to the nonprofits hosting them, "because a lot of them [students] are pretty sheltered, and it takes them a while to understand what the community is really like and who it is that they're working with, and to really gain that level of respect." Even in organizations where racial and class background may play less of a role, the isolated experiences of many white students—from a state still characterized by small rural communities—make them ill-prepared for communicating with people of other cultural backgrounds. In the words of another agency representative:

> [It is a] little difficult for some university students to get in the swing of things—some have never had to deal with a majority population being black and children and dealing with the issues that arise.

Students unfamiliar and uncomfortable with such different community settings may see even relatively easy-to-solve matters like transportation as barriers to service learning, which reinforces their desire to stay in their comfort zones. As one interview participant expressed, "They would rather have their academic life be campus-based." A few interview participants mentioned instances where a student's lack of comfort with diversity revealed a potential danger in service learning, as students who are not reflecting on their own racism and homophobia can have a potentially negative impact on communities:

> It was an instance where we did direct service with [college students], so we had [people] coming in who were struggling with coming-out issues and who were dealing with violence in their dorms, and the LGBT [Lesbian, Gay, Bisexual, & Transgender] center was the one place that they could feel safe and not have to deal with any homophobia. Then we had the service learning student come in and talk about how the reason she was there was because she was uncomfortable with these issues because of her faith, and it really made a lot of people [at the center] uncomfortable. It was just a bad fit.

We can only imagine how the members of that group must have felt. It is important, however, not to blame the student in this case, as she was simply fulfilling a class requirement that challenged students to work with people with whom they were not familiar or comfortable. The insensitivity in this case was on the part of the professor.

Community organizations, of course, do not expect the people they serve to be an expendable source of student enlightenment:

> We will dismiss people for boundary issues, certain attitudes, and beliefs that are inappropriate. People have to be able to come here and expect nondiscriminatory service, whether they are a white supremacist or a lesbian couple. So people who can't show professional objectivity can't volunteer here.

Gender is another form of diversity that challenges community organizations, though they see the issue as mostly a function of the broader culture and higher education. An organization with service learners who are almost exclusively women explains, "It tends to be courses like social work, child welfare, family studies, areas that draw more women." Another organization proposes that "the idea of helping . . . seems to strike a chord as a nurturing thing, which is more a female thing." Overcoming such cultural conditioning, both in the broader culture and within service learning, is difficult but important. The lack of male service learners means a lack of role models in some direct-service situations, illustrated by an interview participant who noted that "the boys tend to have a liking for the males to come here too, even though we don't have as many."

It is hard to overcome the lack of diversity among service learners. The absence of diversity among nonprofit staff and the charity orientation of service learning culture may combine to actually discriminate against students of color who do want to serve their communities. Local fraternities, sororities, and organizations led by students of color engage in significant community work, but they are not receiving course credit for it, and their efforts consequently do not show up as service learning. This is sadly a typical reality, as students of color feel alienated by the nonprofit service sector itself and the charity model of service learning, which they describe as having a "missionary ideology" that imposes outsider values on communities (Weah, Simmons, and Hall, 2000; Simmons and Toole, 2003).

Impacts of Diversity

Being able to work through these dilemmas can have far-ranging benefits. The incorporation of diverse people, with their skills and backgrounds, into social service agencies is viewed as an integral process to building a cohesive and empowered community. Increasing diversity among service learners contributes to this process:

> We have some volunteers that have physical or developmental handicaps, and this is great to see the children learning that anyone can be your friend and you can learn something from that person, and after several weeks or months, they become just a regular face. The children don't see someone like that every day, so it is like going to a small town as an African American or an Asian and the kids at school say you look different, but after a while, we are all the same. This is what we try to teach our kids about tolerance and perception. Everyone is an asset for the success of the activities.

When done properly, this exposure positively affects both service learners and community members. A major impact of diversity among the community population is that the students gain experience that helps them connect more authentically with others (MacGregor, 2003). This is a valuable skill for the development of their future careers and, of course, for living in a global (or local) society (Marullo, 1998). Making diversity a central feature of service learning can build global citizens as the experiences bring people together:

> We also do some religious things, but we don't do them at the same time as our [service activities]. It's important for us not to say, "Here's food, but you also have to have . . . whatever." Being a [Christian] agency, two really good volunteers that we've had, one was Jewish and one was an atheist, and they were great and seemed to enjoy the work they were doing.

Some agency representatives viewed service learning as a chance to blur the lines of server and recipient and confront social inequalities, reinforcing the reciprocal benefits of diversity:

We're encouraging people to share their knowledge, and everyone in the room comes in with experience and with wisdom.

[Service learners] have a different understanding of the issues we deal with, as far as poverty and race and class, but they tend to be white and middle-class students, so we need to talk about that $8,000-a-year average income.

The issues and needs of the clientele is the achievement gap of the disadvantaged population as well as helping kids make good decisions. . . . Our motivation for hosting service learners was to help close the achievement gap. Education helps students learn more along the way.

Some interview participants indicated that when students effectively deal with difference, they can become "role models" for members of the disadvantaged community and "mentors" for kids and youth. While the staff have pretty good secondhand knowledge of client experiences, we do not know from community members themselves how mentoring and service relationships may differ when they are with students who share important social/cultural characteristics, compared to when they do not.

There are actually two issues at play here: (1) the cultural background of the service learner being reflected by the clientele he or she is serving and (2) the level of cultural competency, no matter what the demographics of the service learner. Service learning can address the second of these issues by providing a space for people with different identities and with like identities to share experiences:

Some people have no idea how much it means to have an adult in the classroom, older than them, to sit down and say, "Let's read this magazine if you don't have any homework." Kids don't have that at home, so they are looking for that, and it's not going to be someone who is [way] older than them, but older enough to give them something. That's the whole beauty of being a mentor to these kids.

The best option, of course, is to be able to create a diverse pool of service learners so that the community constituency can provide such role models. A number of staff members from organizations where diversity plays a significant role reported valuing the service learners who themselves had a diverse background. One remarked, "What I've found is that students that are not white have a better understanding of the situation than all of the students that are white." Being asked if race was an important factor in service learners' identities, another organizational representative working in a context serving mostly African American individuals replied that it was indeed important:

> Beyond the student gaining some experience of being in the community, it's good for the neighborhood, particularly working with [a minority student group]. People in the neighborhood get to see people of color going to the university. Good role modeling happens.

Managing a Lack of Diversity

When organizations discover that they can only find mostly white female middle-class service learners, one means of coping is to look for life experiences that indicate the students may be able to at least partially overcome their backgrounds to work effectively with diverse communities (Ward and Wolf-Wendel, 2000). One nonprofit representative tells the story of one of their summer interns, a white male, who fit this category:

> [He] had an experience that woke him up. He was arrested . . . he and his friends were coming out of a bar, and he was arrested for a crime he didn't commit. So when he went through that and was placed in a cell with all black men, he realized how easy it was to be arrested for a crime, and because of his affluence, he was able to go to court and be found innocent. . . . But you realize that if you don't have those resources [for his family to hire a private detective, for example] it could be very easy to be found guilty. . . . When you experience something like that, you just begin to understand what the possibilities

are for other people, given racial issues and also issues of socioeconomics.

In the eyes of one organization representative whose service learners tend to be white female undergraduates, the empathy that such experiences create is important to working across racial and ethnic differences:

> I don't think it has been a barrier. I think if you can walk in their [the community members'] shoes and empathize and know where they have been, whether I am white, black or Hispanic, it does not matter. It is just that that person is there. With the whole bond thing, the cultural barrier is not there.

In addition to relevant life experiences, organizational staff cited other kinds of exposure as being beneficial when working in diverse contexts. These included having similar past work or service experience, marriage or other family relationships with people from other cultures, having spent time abroad, and multilingualism. Spanish and Hmong language ability are important to many organizations in Madison, especially when students have more professional practitioner–oriented roles such as social work and health care.

One of the limitations of this research is that we are hearing community organization representatives and not community members themselves, so white service providers' judgments regarding the effectiveness with which a white service learner can attain empathy may be biased by their own racial privilege. They do notice, however, when students are not making a connection. One interviewee mentioned ways that organizations might be able to be attuned to and manage students' cultural discomfort:

> Sometimes we have seen that maybe they [the service learners] are uncomfortable. Say, with our [clients, who] are a very diverse group, or with the older adults. And maybe that is when we are not making a good match.

Such discomfort, however, can also provide a teachable moment to help students understand how privilege affects them. Paulo Freire

(1985), who made famous the practice of popular education, talks about how white students think of themselves as having a class identity, but not a racial identity, and the importance of confronting their own racial privilege. We have also seen that many staff members feel obligated to make service learning an "eye-opening" life experience from which students can grow and become better citizens. Some interviewees characterize this as a beneficial form of culture shock:

> I have had the occasion where one of the . . . students was very frank about it and told me he was in culture shock, and he was afraid because he had never encountered all of these different children before. And he wasn't afraid for his personal safety or anything like that, but he was afraid of bringing his perceptions about them in and that it would affect them adversely. But so he was looking to grow, as well as them [the clients] learning and growing from him.

Culture shock, of course, also can have negative consequences when students are not properly prepared. For one thing, it can prevent them from making real contact with the community, usually a requirement for successful service learning:

> It was the intellectual, hands-on, computer part of it [that the service learners preferred]. Not the part where you actually have to go out, walk around to businesses . . . or go out and meet clients.

> Sometimes, the ways students are exposed to communities that organizations work with (for example, former prisoners) make them uncomfortable, and this is a very sensitive issue sometimes.

While most organizations greatly value providing real-life learning experiences for service learners, that alone is not enough for some. More importantly, organizations need service learners who are willing to "work with the whole organization," and provide a real benefit to the community:

I'm more interested in those that cross the line in order to engage in some kind of community activity rather than those who
simply study it . . . when not a whole lot is done.

I feel like we're supposed to bring them in, treat them as if
they were part of the staff, bring them close to families even
though they don't have the training, the experience, or the
time to do it, and they're not going to leave us with anything. . . .
And it feels like people want a piece of our family. Students
want, volunteers want, people want to be in there and meet a
real live . . . (homeless) person and get this knowledge and it
feels like almost like a commodity rather than if we say, "Well,
the most helpful thing you could do is X-Y-Z," but that doesn't
give them this exposure.

Organization staff pointed out that such relationships can be "exploitative" or feel "voyeuristic" to the organization's clientele. The above
interviewee emphasizes the need for mutual benefit in such partnerships, saying, "A successful service learning project should not necessarily be direct service." A number of other interview participants
point to this disconnect between what students and organizations consider transformative and worthwhile contributions:

I think some students have a vision in their head, like they will
be coming into the ghetto and it's gonna be really tough, like in
the movies, and then there's these sweet little kids who want to
play Candy Land. And I think some students have felt like,
"Why am I wasting my social work skills playing Candy
Land?" . . . Maybe they see it as valuable, but not a good match
for their skills.

Diversity Training

How do we prepare students for the realities they will encounter in
communities so that they can both learn and contribute to the development of the community? In the discussions we have had with agency
staff since the research findings were presented in draft form, they

have requested diversity training as one of the "standards of service learning" that should be followed by higher education institutions (Stoecker and Tryon, 2007). We agree with the motivation for diversity training, and are uncomfortable with the practice of placing students without preparation in diverse communities solely for the purpose of helping the student overcome stereotypes, rather than to primarily serve the community. Until members of poor and excluded communities are paid as well as professors to confront discriminatory speech and behavior, those students who would present racist or otherwise offensive speech and behaviors must receive adequate education before entering the field. Otherwise, service learning becomes just another form of exploitation by the dominant group.

But so far, we are ill prepared to say what such training would look like. The models in higher education itself are problematic. The discomfort felt by those from dominant groups regarding these hard questions of race, ethnicity, and other types of diversity is evident in our institutions' internal cultural-competency training. In a typical situation, highly paid out-of-town experts are brought in to facilitate training at the behest of the Human Resource Department. Often, and ironically, this training is stratified by position—grouping together directors, vice chancellors, and deans for one training, followed by sessions for the faculty, and then for the staff. Already, this defeats the purpose of helping those in the dominant group (white male highly paid PhDs) see the perspectives of subordinated groups. Some of this training does contain moments of eye-opening revelation about deep-seated issues, such as when students or staff are given space to describe instances of discrimination or feeling unwelcome at an institution that has marketed itself as a good place for students of color. But those revelations provide no mechanism for creating solutions and thus might serve only to alienate the people involved. Despite good intentions, when training participants are not integrated across the institutional hierarchy—including students and staff—new attitudes and behaviors do not internalize and translate back to the everyday work situations, and old habits hold sway.

We may be equally unsuccessful in developing cultural sensitivity training for students. Aside from the occasional film or afternoon training, there is a relative absence of such training among both the higher education institutions that sponsor service learning and the community organizations that host them. Those of us in the fields of sociology, anthropology, and specialized race and ethnic studies know that even when we spend four or more years educating students about race, class, sex, and other forms of diversity, we sometimes only see a dent in attitudes.

There are several cultural-competency training models, such as that used by the YWCA Racial Justice Institute (YWCA Madison, 2008; see also Valenciano, 2007; Allen, 2002), along with some written guidelines put out by the Southern Poverty Law Center (Holladay, 2006), among others. However, it is important to pay attention to the way this training is carried out. Even cultural-competency training and theory can be approached from too much of a privilege model, and can do as much damage as no training. The challenge facing cultural diversity training programs is that, almost by necessity, they must be based on stereotypes. Helping a white upper-middle-class young female service learner understand what it means to be a poor middle-aged African American male usually defaults to describing the "average" experience of a person occupying those categories. The problem is, that average person doesn't exist in reality, and a student who goes out with only enough training to understand the stereotype often will add insult to injury. In addition, we struggle over just how to portray the average person of the combination of categories—as survivor or victim (Watts-Jones, 2002). We want students to understand that the problem behaviors they see in many community settings are the results of deeply structured forces of oppression, exploitation, and exclusion. And we want students also to see and understand the strengths of a community. A student who works with an alcohol treatment program in an indigenous community context, for example, needs enough education on that community's culture to be able to see its continuing resiliency. There are rural regions where community members' unfamiliarity with, or distrust of, higher education can make it very difficult for students even to enter the community and do any meaningful work, requiring that faculty and community organization staff do much more preparation than might be the case in other settings. We need to do that in ways that do not unduly burden community resources or assume no-cost educational services from community members.

The necessary reliance by some cultural-competency training programs on helping students understand the broad categories of race has produced critiques. Mitchell (2007), for example, suggests that labels on any group are harmful, that people in dominant cultures should spend more time focusing on individuals instead of groups, and that training would be unneeded if people lived in a more integrated environment from childhood. He emphasizes: "Don't value diversity, value human beings." Such critics emphasize the more basic skills of relationship-building dialogue practices as a way to get past cultural stereotypes. Appreciative inquiry (Cooperrider and Srivastva, 1987; Appreciative Inquiry Commons, 2007), which encourages dialogue without judgments; study and learning diversity circles (Everyday Democracy, 2005; Fond du Lac Diversity Circles, n.d.); and a number of other practices can accomplish such goals. The problem with this approach is the opposite of cultural-competency training. Appreciating the experience of another individual, without having a deeper understanding of the institutional oppressions of race, gender, class, ability, age, and other structural realities, may also produce inaccurate stereotypes. Participants generalize from the experiences of one person to entire groups haphazardly, with no in-depth understanding of how race, class, and other structural oppressions may shape an individual's experience.

A third approach to the issue is to focus on self-understanding as much as on the "other." Rhoads (1997), for example, says that "for students to walk a mile in another's shoes, they must first be aware of their own position in society and what it brings to the service relationship. In the service learning context, positionality is about the social histories students bring to their service." Historically, this has been one of the goals of the reflection component that many service learning proponents recommend (Bringle and Hatcher, 1999). In many cases, however, reflection is used only after the service learning commences. What happens, though, if we make reflection part of diversity training, and institute it long before students go into the field? It is possible that we may have to build students' self-awareness before they can become aware of those who may be different from them in significant ways. We need to educate students in the structural dynamics of class, race, sex and gender, ability, and other structural divisions, and ask them to reflect on that knowledge in relation to their own lives. This preparatory education/reflection process allows students to understand the role of social structure in shaping people's lives, and the role of the community, family, and individuals in mediating or resisting those influences.

It can also make students aware of the common causes of different forms of inequality and oppression, and help them see how different people's experiences may be connected. This is the classic process proposed by C. Wright Mills (1959) of understanding the intersection of biography and history. This self-awareness process helps students practice with the categories in a way that allows them to see both their general application and the variation that individual circumstances add to them. Perhaps then students can think about others both in terms of the general categories and each community's and individual's uniqueness, and consciously understand the process of listening for and analyzing the intersection of history and biography in the community context.

Diversity training, then, may be better described as a process of understanding than as a substitution of knowledge. How do we help students look for the influence of structural forces, and how do we help them look for community, family, and individual strategies that respond to those forces? How do we help students practice that process and how do we set standards for their ability to implement that process before allowing them to enter the field? Since we are not aware of any such programs (indeed, we know of few diversity training programs of any kind), we do not know the answers to these questions. Perhaps others will consider this an opportunity. We may need to integrate these types of diversity and reflection activities through the curriculum. We may need immersion experiences in protected settings. But we certainly need to think bigger and more creatively than we have been.

Conclusion: Building a "Culture of Diversity"

We are seeing some change in culture, as service learning begins to confront both the issue of diversity and the inequity between academy and community in the service learning relationship. Some service learning centers have titled themselves centers of "community-based learning" or "education" rather than "service" centers. The Center for Urban Research and Learning at Loyola University Chicago, and the Trent Centre for Community-Based Education in Peterborough, Canada, for example, explicitly avoid putting "service" in their titles to promote more equitable relationships between community and academy. Of course, a name alone does not prevent service learning from causing harm, nor does shifting from a charity to "change" mission. The entire system of oppression and discrimination within which service learning exists includes not only the higher education institutions that control it and the nonprofit organizations that mediate it, but also the structure of power in society that circumscribes it.

The diversity issues facing students, organizations, and communities are interlinked, reflecting many socioeconomic conditions of the wider society. Service learning students often are emotionally and intellectually unprepared for working with people who do not share a similar background, especially as it relates to aspects of class and race. Unleashing students on communities who differ from them in important characteristics, without proper preparation and reflection with their professors, can reinforce students' negative stereotypes and do more harm than good to intergroup relations in society. Conversely, when students are prepared in ways that help them understand they are not just there to help but also to learn from the strengths of people unlike them, students can also be part of the solution to the racial and class divides that plague our country.

But bridging the diversity divide is not the only strategy for dealing with it. Many organizations desire service learners who share the racial, class, gender, and ability demographics of the communities themselves, serving as role models for youth and peers. As members of historically excluded communities can build their sense of self-esteem and power in free spaces controlled by the community and relatively insulated from outsiders, they are then better able to assert themselves as equals in relationships with dominant groups (Evans and Boyte, 1992). Students who can be seen as members of, or significantly similar to, their host communities, however, are in short supply in higher education. Broad structural issues need to be addressed in order to change that condition, not just in service learning programs and environments of higher education but also within the national culture as a whole.

These issues are beyond the scope of this report, but deserve more attention in other settings. We need a dialogue about ways to increase diversity and an appreciation for diversity among service learning students. We need to better understand why students of color are not attracted to fields that typically engage in service learning. We need to create systems that enable people of color and others who may have significant knowledge based on life experience rather than formal education, and have been doing volunteer work for no college credit, to earn a certificate that would place them on a level playing field with college-trained interns. Then, when positions in community agencies become available, such individuals will be more competitive. The people we interviewed and those who send service learners to them cannot even imagine such possibilities.

When we effectively address the issue of diversity, community organizations will have more capacity to provide opportunities for historically disadvantaged and excluded people, and diversity will become both more visible and more celebrated, breaking the cycle of exclusion. One of the paths toward responding to the dilemma of diversity is in the process of service learning itself. Vogelgesang, Drummond, and Gilmartin (2003) describe four cases where community organizations were intimately involved in the design of the service learning programs themselves, right down to the construction of the syllabi, to maintain a focus on diversity issues. The perspective of community organization staff can inform a dynamically different approach to the service learning practice, adding value to the experience for all the people involved in it.

8 One Director's Voice

It's a small office suite, just three rooms shared by two organizations, three staff people, a cadre of volunteers and service learners, an occasional house pet, and stacks of paper, markers, and other tools of the trade.

It is the circus that many small nonprofits are, yet there is an air of joyous community and of success. In four years, the Grassroots Leadership College (GLC), a nonprofit organization in Madison, Wisconsin, that specializes in teaching community organizing skills to older teens and adults and supporting their ongoing community work, has boasted more than three hundred graduates from four program areas and the development of a volunteer base of more than fifty. What does this mean for service learners? What role does service learning play in this success?

It all comes down to one motto: "Everyone a learner, everyone a teacher, everyone a leader." That's it. That's the radical view of the world that changes how community works and shuffles the balance of power. It gives service learners ownership of their work and an opportunity to really engage as members of the community—not just college students who may be new to the place in which they now live—and sparks the creative nature of community members.

It's just that easy and just that hard.

ganizing a new neighborhood association, she asks a lot of questions, encouraging Sue to really dig deep within her own experiences for answers. She listens. She shares her experiences, being careful not to overshadow Sue's. She asks even more questions and keeps listening, drawing out Sue's innate wisdom from having lived in the experience she's seeking to organize around. Sometimes, Tamika hears something from Sue that changes a preconceived notion she held about Sue's neighborhood or she learns about a new successful organizing tactic she might use in her own neighborhood. She came into the situation defined as a leader in her coach role, recognized herself as a teacher, and allowed herself the opportunity to learn. Those choices helped Sue learn not just from Tamika, but also from herself, strengthening her belief in her own ability to lead. Sue is able to go back to her neighborhood and use what she learned from Tamika and from herself to build a successful group and to pass on her new skills to others.

Coach Two, we'll name Steve. Steve sees himself as a teacher and leader in his coach role, and perceives the developing leader, Laurie, as the learner. Steve is really interested in Laurie's project, coordinating a meal site for homeless families with children. Laurie shares her thoughts about holding the meals on Saturdays at a small church in her neighborhood and having toys and games for the kids and a playtime with volunteers after the meal that would allow the parents a chance to have a break. Steve happens to know a few children's entertainers and has a connection to a large community center. He thinks, "Wow, this project could really be something!" and starts making a few calls. In no time, he's lined up a juggler, a clown, a magician, and a musician, each of whom are willing to donate their time one Saturday a month, and he's reserved the community center for the dates. Laurie's project could be called a big success or one could look a little deeper and see that Laurie has become a worker bee in the effort that she had begun as the leader. She's lost her role in determining the direction of the effort. She's been given a workload that she hasn't agreed to, and she's lost ownership of her own idea.

In Tamika and Sue's case, the vision and mission have been fulfilled. In Steve and Laurie's scenario, we've all lost something. Steve didn't take the opportunity to learn from Laurie. Laurie didn't get to see herself as a leader, to build her own networks, or to learn new skills. The GLC didn't succeed in fulfilling the idea that we are all learners, teachers, and leaders.

Sometimes, the goal for a service learner shouldn't simply be to get a project done, whether that is in the sense here of coaching a developing leader to a project's end or directly doing a project for a nonprofit. The learning comes in the process, not in the outcome. Our service learners have benefited when their class requires some way of analyzing their experience throughout the semester. We also attempt to offer that experience in our conversations and evaluation of the service learner's work.

At the end of the semester, Sue and Tamika may or may not have a new neighborhood association that is functioning. They will likely have a base that will become a neighborhood association, but perhaps more importantly, they've both learned something about themselves, their abilities, and how to effectively lead in a way that they can apply to many future projects.

Moving the Work Forward

A wise community organizer once told me the goal of an organizer should be to organize him- or herself out a job. Our success is evident when those we sought to organize claim their power and create their own win. That only happens when our to-do lists are more than simply a list of tasks. Our work plans need to become a strategy map of sorts, charting our route. Before taking on a service learner, it's important to think about where that person fits on the map.

Whether we are community organizers, human service organizations, or other forms of nonprofits, we generally share the goal of making the place where we live better in some way. How do we engage service learners in that process?

Sometimes we need a person to stuff envelopes and sometimes we need him or her to organize a press conference. Both of those things are valid tasks for a service learner, as long as they fit within the organizational mission and vision, and as long as they are instrumental in moving toward final goals.

Our role, as mentors, includes helping the service learner understand the map that we are using to move forward, remembering that we've been reading this map for a long time, and they may never have had a chance before to delve into understanding organizing strategies.

Herein lies a challenge. Can we take the time and energy to hold the hand of the service learner to show him or her how our world of work operates? Are we open to the possibility that the service learner might show us where we took a wrong turn?

A favorite early task for volunteers and service learners alike at the GLC is to proofread press releases and grant requests. It's a good tool for the learner to start to understand the organization. It's a good tool for us to make sure that our grant requests and news releases aren't filled with jargon that people outside of the organization aren't familiar with. It's also an easy way to encourage new learners to share ideas and feedback by engaging them in conversation: "If you were on the foundation board, what would inspire you to fund this proposal? What are we missing?" and "If you were the editor, would you print this release? What other information would you need?"

Remaining open to the suggestions here is both a challenge and a joy. Sometimes new eyes see things we missed and strengthen the work, and sometimes the ideas shared show us where we need to do more educating.

Again, this comes back to analytical thinking skills. In this age where many students come into higher education having spent twelve years learning how to answer test questions with the "correct" response, it's difficult to teach them to think on their own in a situation that doesn't have a single "right" answer. It is, however, essential if they are going to benefit the organization in which they work.

Faculty can support nonprofits by getting students to really think about their goals in the service learning experience, by analyzing what they are learning constantly throughout the process, and encouraging them to figure out how this experience is affecting them right now and how it will impact their future. It is the great challenge of higher education to get students to think for themselves.

Once students come to trust in their own creative thinking and build a commitment to the organization in which they work, they are an invaluable resource. Our participants love the students who coordinate our recruitment efforts, help design our programs, and coordinate our alumni support. As a small organization with a limited budget, we couldn't do our work without them.

Resources and Relationship Building

Having the energy and the resources to build a relationship with the service learner is essential. Without it, there's no guarantee that the results will even be recognizable, much less beneficial to the organization.

Several years ago, the Grassroots Leadership College agreed to be a project site for a business class. We would provide an opportunity for a group of undergraduates to draft a marketing plan. As the typical overworked director, I thought, "Great! We could really use a few folks who have the time to sit down and figure out how we can better market our work and move the organization forward. That would really take a load off of me!"

Early in the semester, I met with the students for several hours, guiding them through all the aspects of the organization and sharing ideas with them. Weeks passed and I heard nothing more from them. I couldn't reach them. I e-mailed the faculty person and heard nothing. At the end of the semester, I received a packet. It was our business plan. I read it and laughed. I could hardly recognize the organization that they thought they worked with.

We got nothing. The students, unfortunately, maybe got even less. They cheated themselves of an opportunity to learn about marketing in a real-world setting and to better understand how a small business works. The faculty member, the students, and I all missed an opportunity to enhance our learning and build our connections to the community.

Today, I think twice before taking on any class projects. When we do decide to support a class project, it's because we've already begun to get to know the faculty member and trust that person. We set up a system of accountability, so I know who to call if there is a problem and we know how to work things out together. Early on, the students and I work out a contract that spells out what I expect of them and what they can expect of me. We refer back to that contract throughout the time we have together to help us stay on task and evaluate our relationship and our strategies.

It makes a significant difference for us to have that connection.

A more recent interaction with a class group looks like this. We've worked with a group of first-year students. First I came to class, along with other nonprofits, and told them about the opportunities we had available. Then their teacher guided them through a process of choosing the organization that made the most sense for their learning goals. Soon after, the faculty member assigned a program staff person to be our primary contact. That person supplied me with a list of contact information for the students, as well as his contact information should I have any concerns. I then began the process of biweekly meetings with the students. Monthly, I could expect an e-mail or call from the program staff person just to check in. In class, the students shared journals and discussion of the project. The faculty person called me immediately when she learned from the students that they were feeling a little lost in the beginning. She and I were able to communicate directly to figure out together how to support the students. I got the project I needed. The students learned a great deal. And, I think that faculty person and I will continue to work together.

Maintaining the Work

Working in a small nonprofit that depends largely on volunteer labor sometimes means reinventing the wheel, modifying or sometimes discontinuing programs if volunteers move on, or it can mean staff stepping in and adding to their workload. What work can stop? How can the work be done after this service learner leaves? How can the service learner create a legacy by developing the tools for his or her work to continue?

Service learners and volunteers want to know that their work is valuable. They want to feel a part of the organization in a long-term way, even if their contracted commitment is only short term. It's to the benefit of the organization that these often short-term workers feel a long-term connection. They are, after all, potential future donors, members, allies, and recruiters.

The connections that service learners build with organizations and their ability to do beneficial work depend on the relationships that faculty build with nonprofits. Our successes have been born in those places where we have found common ground. The faculty who ask us what we need and are available to work with are an absolute joy. They are the gardeners growing student minds in fertile gardens. The ones who send students out to find whatever they can are casting seeds into the wind. Some will find a fertile place to grow, many will not.

Coming Full Circle—Evaluating and Setting Expectations for the Next Service Learning Opportunity

Every step of the way includes evaluation. The end of a service learning opportunity is no exception. It is key to future success to ask the learner about his or her experience. What did the person learn? How did the relationship succeed? What didn't work as well for the learner? It's just as important to ask others involved in the experience. Who did the learner work with? What was their experience? How did the learning opportunity work for the organization? Was it a help or just another piece of work for the staff? What did the staff learn?

We are all learners, teachers, and leaders. We just have to give ourselves the opportunity to fill each of these roles. It's hard. Sometimes the work spins by so quickly, it's easy to skip this important step. Without it, however, the challenges build and the successes shrink. It's the evaluation process that brings us back to:

- How does service learning fit within our mission and vision?
- How will this relationship and project move our work forward?
- What resources do we have to give to this relationship?
- What resources do we have to maintain and build the work beyond this learner's term with the organization? Is it sustainable?
- What are our expectations for the experience? Are those expectations shared by the faculty and the learner?

It's that evaluation that prepares us for the next go-around.

9 Principles for Success in Service Learning—the Three Cs

Dadit Hidayat, Samuel Pratsch, and Randy Stoecker

This project grew from the concerns of community agency staff that service learning wasn't delivering all it promised for its host communities. So we set out to better understand those concerns, but we wanted to do more than simply list them. We also wanted enough information to begin developing a service learning model that would better serve communities and their organizations. Doing so has led us through a two-step process. The first step appears in this chapter: deriving principles that guide effective service learning from the sixty-seven interviews with community organization staff. The next chapter builds on those principles, and a series of subsequent meetings with community organization staff, to suggest new frameworks for the practice of service learning.

We have talked about the issues of finding and recruiting students, coping with short-term service learning, managing service learners under often less-than-ideal circumstances, compensating for the lack of diversity among service learners, and developing and maintaining good relationships with the higher education side of the partnership. Here, we begin pulling together what we heard does seem to work and address the question of what constitutes a successful service learning experience from the community's perspective.

Our analysis leads us to propose the three Cs of service learning that serve the big "C"—community—of the service learning partnership, and likely will serve the students as well. The three Cs are:

- Commitment
- Communication
- Compatibility

Based on the organization representatives we spoke with, the success of a service learning project depends in large part upon the level of commitment made by both the academic and community partners to developing and carrying out a successful project; the effectiveness of communication between the professor, student, and organization prior to and during the project; and the compatibility—in terms of cultural understanding, knowledge, and professional skills—of the service learning program and the student with the community organization site. Not every success story we heard about shared all of these ingredients in equal measure, and their presence are not guarantors of success. However, according to these organization representatives, they seem to be the most fundamental principles governing service learning success. We have seen them come up again and again in our research, including in Chapter 8, written by the director of the Grassroots Leadership College.

Here we develop these three components as principles to guide service learning. And in contrast to the previous chapters, which focused mainly on what was not working, we now look at what community organization staff believe does work.

Commitment

Commitment may be the most fundamental of the three Cs, for without a commitment to the community, there will be neither the energy to maintain good communication nor the will to develop training and screening mechanisms to assure compatibility.

There are, of course, many service learning professionals who are committed to the idea of service learning. That commitment, however, has been mostly to the institution and the student, and not so much to the community and its organizations, at least based on what we have learned in this project. We are talking here about developing a serious commitment to the community and its development, which is significantly different.

How might a full commitment to the community make service learning look different? First, there will be a commitment to developing longer-term service learning. As we detail in Chapter 4, short-term service learning creates problems for many agencies. More than a third of the organizations linked the success of service learning projects to faculty and students making a long-term commitment to the community and building a strong relationship between the student, professor, and organization. Many times, we heard some version of, "We would like people that can make a long-term commitment":

> If that was an ongoing service relationship, then people could be involved in direct service, perhaps [with a greater length of time]. . . . If service learning became even broader to be an ongoing requirement, over a year or two, that would open up some really interesting potential in terms of students' ability to grow within a program, and strengthen connection within the community.

Most of these organizations thought that service learning commitments should be at least a year and some of the organizations wanted it to be at least two years. Most recognized that a semester is too short a time for the student to make a substantial impact. One indicator of a serious commitment would be faculty who are willing to work outside of the academic world's artificial, fifteen-week semester calendar:

> It would be interesting and really good for us to engage some of our service learners for a longer period of time, since some of them are only a semester. That's really just enough time to get to understand the program a little bit.

> One of the things I have always tried to do with service learning programs is to find projects where the project can be spread over a year and half, perhaps two years even, each time you get new energy into it. This is an important point; you have

to understand that one semester is a short period of time and by the time the students get up to speed and really get going, it is the end of the semester.

Beyond a programmatic commitment to service learning, community organization staff are also looking for students to make serious commitments to the agency and its host community. The variability in commitment from students makes service learning a highly unpredictable investment for community organizations. Even when an agency sets up the same project for several students, it can come out entirely differently for each, depending on the students' personal characteristics. Almost all of the community organizations said that the student's work ethic, including his or her personality, is significant in determining the success of the project. Service learners must have a clear interest of their own in the project and a passion for the issues being addressed by the organization. Community organization staff believe that, when the service learner is intrinsically motivated, he or she will have a stronger commitment to do quality work. Sometimes that motivation is quite specific, and sometimes it is more amorphous:

> The most success has been when the student comes in and they know they want to get something specific out of it.

> The interest of the person in the work that we do, and their just positive energy that they bring to the work.

Most community organization staff understand the challenges of being a college student. However, they still expect to see a different level of motivation from service learners because they are not only learning but also giving service to the community. Community organization staff really want service learners to make a commitment to the organization's work, and not just to meeting course requirements:

> I think it's partly to do with motivation. If it's just a course requirement, they're probably not going to stick around, but if they've integrated it, there's a reason internally why they're doing it, and they might continue. It's pretty obvious right away who's doing it because they have to, and then we almost

wish that person could just find something else to do . . . because it's a lot of work to make those matches . . . schedules, etcetera, so it's frustrating when that person doesn't really want to be there. . . . And it hasn't happened a lot, but it does happen.

The individual character of a service learner is another key factor of success from the community organization's point of view. Most interview participants emphasized the need for service learners who are genuinely interested, can be relied on, have effective communication and listening skills, and feel a sense of ownership for their service learning work:

> [The students'] personalities were the type where they took a lot of initiative and just really dove into it. I could tell that they really felt strongly about what we're doing as an organization and their role with all of that. And that went a long way too, it being a beneficial experience for them and for us because they had that same drive about helping our clients.

> Because once they feel that they have ownership of the project and what they're doing, they're going to take pride in that and want to continue on doing it. Because service learning is not just the whole process, but what happens after the process of them being involved in their communities.

Behind the organization staff's hopes for a higher-level commitment from students are their concerns that too many students can't make the most basic commitments. As we have seen, a number of organizations have concerns about the reliability of students even to show up at a service learning site. Despite the fact that the service learner has regular classes and activities outside of class, community organizations believe it is essential for service learners to maintain regular working hours:

> I think a regular schedule is a really important thing. . . . Although I liked her as an individual, it felt like it was a lot of work to try and have something for her to do and because of the

irregular schedule it made it more difficult and, in that case, it was probably more of a burden than what we got from her.

In some cases, students also need to be flexible enough to change their schedules when public meetings or community events occur.

Finally, at the most basic level of relationship is the organization staff's hope that those on the academic side will minimally make a commitment to the practical activity of actually carrying out the project. This often includes making a commitment on paper through a memorandum of understanding (see Gonzalez, 2007). Eight of the organizations interviewed declared that formalizing the relationship with a contract was critical because it clarified the commitments for everyone involved in the project. According to the staff of one organization:

> In our experience, we have formal agreement from the get-go as to what the expectations are, both from the student's perspective as well as the organization's and the faculty's.

Another agency has a contract covering the entire service learning process:

> We have our own student contract where we ask students, "What are your goals, what are you committing to do, what are we committing to do, and how are we going to check in and evaluate that?"

We learn more about the specifics of such contracts in Chapter 10.

Communication

The second C, communication, is often an indicator of the level of commitment of the faculty and students in a service learning relationship. At least twenty-nine organizations in this study emphasized that faculty involvement, characterized by effective and timely communication, was fundamental to the success of service learning:

> We [the organization] need to know what our needs are and we need to know what our limitations are for doing this active teaching and supervision. The students need to know what their

realistic time constraints are. And the professor needs to know what the assignment is. And we all need to communicate those things with each other. So if there is a link in that communication that is broken, it [the service learning experience] seems to all fall apart and not be a good experience for all involved. Things that have gone wrong in the past have been a breaking of a link in the communication chain.

It is evident from this statement that effective communication enables all the participants in the service learning project to be clear about their expectations. It also enables the organization to better manage the service learner, as another organization representative points out:

I would say that it's when we, as a community organization, are in direct contact with the professor . . . making sure that we were both on the same page, and understood what each other's expectations were so the same message was conveyed to the students by both.

Effective communication not only aids in clarifying expectations and managing the service learning project but also provides opportunities for the organization to learn about service learning. In the words of one organization staff member:

For myself, getting educated about what service learning is from the academic perspective . . . it really helped to clarify . . . the roles within the university and the community.

Ultimately, effective communication is about the student-organization-professor triad, one-to-one and all-to-one. So, along with all three meeting together, the organization and student need to talk on a regular basis:

Ideally, I like to meet with [the students] every few weeks and just kind of do an ongoing "touch-base": "How's it going? What are you getting, what aren't you getting? Where are you? This is where I see you going."

And the organization staff and professor need to interact. One key to effective communication is when the professor makes the effort to visit the site of the organization in the community:

> Yeah [I felt like I had a strong relationship to the professor]. It was interesting how he came out first and really got to know me and what we were doing . . . and I think that was extremely valuable.

Two other staff members emphasize the importance of the faculty taking some initiative to learn about the community and the organization:

> Leave the campus. I think it is important to faculty members to spend time with [the] community to see what happens, build relationships, and make a good fit. This probably needs to be done before the project starts to develop the partnership.

> A couple of times I've gotten calls from professors saying, "How did things go?" The marketing group that did work on promoting our event, the professor actually came to the event and he talked to us. He really made an effort to be there and to ask questions . . . and the students were there as well. So I thought that was really neat.

One organization representative thinks that face-to-face time including all three parties is important, no matter where it occurs:

> So places where the professor, myself, and the student have sat down and worked things out have worked out the best. As far as structurally, the more formal the better. . . . It almost always works best when it's face-to-face. We all tend to think of phone and e-mail as helpful tools, but it's my experience that they're very limited helpful tools. And they're best for conveying meeting times and often just some factual information . . . but if we're talking about what somebody found out or what's been accomplished, that's got to be face-to-face.

What is the substance of such communication? Thirteen organizations emphasized how important it is for everyone involved to have clear expectations for any service learning project:

Having a clear expectation of what the service learning goals are, across the board—that's myself, the student, the professor . . . is critical to the success of the service learning project.

One organization staff member believes this is important because:

If we don't strongly know what we're going to do, the student is going to flounder a little bit . . . so when we have clear-cut goals [we have better success].

Here, again, some form of written agreement can help make everyone's expectations clear.

Compatibility

The third C of successful service learning, compatibility, is somewhat of an art. It can also be compared to those memory games for kids, where you turn cards over and try to remember where you saw the one matching what you've just turned over. Or, think of it as the pieces in a giant jigsaw puzzle.

Fourteen organizations recognized the importance of a good fit between the goals of the organization and students. They expressed this idea of fit in a variety of ways:

When a person comes . . . we tell them about all the different programs and we try and make it a good match for them as well as a good match for us.

If what they're offering is something that we could benefit from.

I think that what makes it successful is that we each come out of it feeling like we've gotten something, that it's a win-win situation for the student as well as the organization.

[Having a service learner] is both valuable to the organization, in terms of additional things accomplished that we would perhaps have not been able to do, while at the same time being a learning experience to the student so that they get enough out of it to come out of it feeling like they have learned something.

It is not always easy to create that mutual benefit, as one staff person states:

> We try to be flexible. We try to identify projects that are going to be helpful to us but also meaningful to them, so sometimes we have to be quite flexible in what we do in order to meet those needs.

This concept of mutuality of fit emphasizes that service learning cannot be just about the student, even when there is pressure to serve students first. In cases where the student has an interest in fitting the service learning work into his or her own professional or personal development, it is all the more important that the organization, the student, and the professor be clear about their expectations and motivations for participating in the service learning project. Many service learning experiences are useful as resume builders and provide insight into possible career choices, but to insist on things being set up a certain way only for the student's gain is exploitative of the community agency and its constituency.

Another way that agency staff think about the fit between the organization and the service learner involves personality characteristics:

> The other thing is they have a certain amount of competitiveness. Meaning, they take on challenges. If one method is not working to teach a math problem, they try another route. Maybe it is not competitiveness, but persistence. I believe they have an innate ability to work with people or they don't. I don't believe it is something you can develop. Maybe you can develop it, but you certainly cannot create it [from nothing]. These people are usually people who have always been involved in helping people.

As discussed in Chapter 3, a number of agencies interview students to determine whether they will be a good fit. Others try to provide students with as much information about the organization as they can, so the student has the opportunity to determine how good a fit the project would be with his or her expectations. But the issue of fit is not just about whether the student fits the organization. It is also about whether the entire service learning program fits the needs of the community and its organizations. Nine organizations made the statement that a service learning project is successful if the project fits into their programs:

> If somebody calls and says, "We'd like to come out and volunteer," . . . and they say, "We have to paint," . . . and we've just painted everything . . . , they could put another coat on, but it really wasn't necessary.

Of course, the issue of compatibility is not just about the compatibility of the service learning program with the agency's mission, or of the service learner as an individual with the culture and work of the community organization. It is also about the conditions under which programs are designed and service learners are trained, affecting how well either will fit with community organizations. Currently, the institution's schedule and the professor's priorities determine the level of training that service learners are provided with, as well as how and when they receive it. The training can be particularly important:

> [What would help is] some sort of "boot camp" about how to "be" in an office . . . recognizing that this is a more informal space than a lot of others, certainly compared to corporate internships, but still, people have full days of work and need to get them done.

The question of compatibility, then, takes us deep into the history and institutional motivations of service learning and of higher education institutional culture itself. The literature has already established that there is a lack of compatibility between academy and community in terms of schedules, deadlines, and priorities (Strand et al., 2003). It has not traced the effects of these incompatibilities to their ultimate conclusion. There are consequences when there is not compatibility, such as:

- A community organization loses nearly its entire student volunteer base, who are supporting the organization's after-school program, because the local schools run until mid-June, but the university gets out in mid-May.

- A meeting doesn't happen because the service learner who was supposed to send out the reminder notices had a paper deadline that took priority.
- A child is left wondering what's wrong because the college student who was mentoring him or her just stopped showing up one day.

Taking the issue of compatibility seriously can unravel the current structure of higher education. Service learning that serves communities requires, first, that the service learning program operate on the community calendar. That means service learners and their sponsoring faculty being available over the holidays for those organizations working with constituencies who are particularly vulnerable then, for example, or beyond spring graduation for those working with school programs that extend beyond that time. The attitude that partial service is better than nothing perpetuates the problematic perception that the community is there to serve the institution's needs.

Ultimately, service learning that truly fits the community would be based on a yearlong model of higher education. One unique institution, Trent University in Canada, as we note in Chapter 4, has a strong service learning program that emphasizes students engaging in community-designed projects and also offers a full academic year of courses. While still breaking for holidays and summer, the Trent courses run from fall through spring, allowing students to spend much more time on projects than during the more common semester or trimester course.

Second, service learning that serves communities needs to be designed around community issues. This means that service learning courses may need to be designed and scheduled not a year before they are offered, but only one to a few months before, as the severity of community conditions and issues shift without warning. Some are experimenting with the "flash seminar" model of service learning (Stoecker, 2008; Cutforth and Stocking, 2005). Indeed, the community-based research project that led to this book was based on a flash seminar created only two months before the start of classes. That means dramatically changing the course-scheduling process to accommodate large numbers of last-minute courses for both faculty and students.

Third, service learning that serves communities needs to provide a very different kind of education for students. Communication skills, professional skills, specialized practice skills, and others should not be just two-hour training add-ons, but a part of the curriculum for service learners who are going to do more good than harm. This can be particularly challenging for research-intensive and liberal arts institutions that offer few skills-based courses. Such an educational milieu may also require a new breed of student who seeks service learning not for a line on their resume, but more to provide real service. Those students also must be open enough to learn from people who often have different racial and class backgrounds, and consequently less formal education than they do. Service learning, therefore, may become an activity that students will have to apply for, rather than just another requirement for them to meet. Of course, we must provide a curriculum that develops students who can successfully apply for such opportunities.

And, of course, these changes reverberate into the way we prepare and evaluate faculty. Our graduate programs must prepare future faculty in how to develop and maintain community relationships, how to run a meeting, how to link research to action, and a variety of other skills that are considered irrelevant or are assumed to be easy. It may even require developing a new breed of faculty, and a new paradigm of tenure and promotion guidelines and workload rules. Far beyond those institutions that simply recognize community service as part of the portfolio, we may need to develop guidelines that recognize a faculty member who teaches no traditional courses, publishes no traditional journal articles, and provides no traditional professional service, but instead is engaged with bringing large numbers of students into the field to do effective work with large numbers of community organizations.

Conclusion

This project shows the results of our current institution-centric version of service learning: too many organizations left dissatisfied with the outcomes of service learning and too many communities underserved. There were a number of organizations who would not talk to us for this project. We heard indirectly that at least some of them had such negative experiences with service learning that not only did they not want to talk about it, but they wouldn't even consider any further trials with the practice. This is the service learning dialectic. If we continue the current model that serves students at the expense of communities, we risk alienating more and more community organizations until the practice of service learning itself is threatened. This is an area where an alarm should be raised to preserve the sustainability of this practice—it's important to ensure that the community organizations don't feel taken advantage of, lest they decide eventually that hosting service learners is not worth the hassle.

It is imperative that those of us privileged enough to attend college, or to be entrusted with serving its students, also feel obligated to serve the community, not as vanguard leaders or charity providers but as true partners. We're all interrelated and interdependent, not self-contained in academic or community vacuums. The oft-quoted statement coined by an Australian Aboriginal activist group and often attributed to Aboriginal elder Lila Watson (Northland Poster Collective, 2006), "If you have come here to help me, then you are wasting your time. But if you have come because your liberation is bound up with mine, then let us work together," applies to service learning perhaps better than to any other partnership we can create.

The community organizations that we interviewed engaged with us in developing a set of community standards for service learning, which they hope will be taken up by faculty and administrators and used to help prepare and implement better service learning projects. We have been circulating their draft of this "Standards for Service Learning" brochure at several conferences, teaching and learning symposia, and throughout much of the community. It has so far been very well received by all parties. You can read our elaboration of that brochure in Chapter 10. In the meantime, agencies in Madison, Wisconsin, continue to host service learners because they really need the help. Many also value the opportunity to be informal teachers in a real-life setting that can transform students to become better-engaged citizens, or to even begin lifelong relationships with particular nonprofits or causes.

Some of you may think that community organizations, and we as their supporters, are setting the bar too high. These are, after all, students. We should not expect them to exhibit the skills of trained employees. There is a tacit understanding among most nonprofits that when dealing with unpaid help, be it service learners or well-meaning volunteers, things do not always work smoothly, and that's just the nature of the nonprofit beast. However, if higher educational institutions can even begin to incorporate some of these suggestions and internalize organizations' preferences in their course planning, relationship building, and preparation of service learners, it will go a long way toward better practice of service learning. The result will be a true "win-win" situation that benefits not only the learning objectives of the student and teaching goals of their professor, but does more good than harm to the community they purport to serve.

ow do we actually implement the three Cs of commitment, communication, and compatibility? What do all four parties—faculty, students, service learning offices, and community organizations—have to do to make service learning as successful for the community as it is for the student?

Remember that this project began in the fall of 2005 with a few community organizations expressing their concerns about how service learning was not fully meeting their needs. By the spring of 2006, we had sixty-seven interviews organized into seven drafted chapters of material. But it was not enough for us to simply write a report and go home; this was, after all, an action research project. If we were going to find problems, we were also going to figure out what we could do about them and act. So in May 2006, we organized a community event with the core group of nonprofits guiding the effort. The students presented poster boards of their research, and organizations told stories of their experiences with service learning—like those described by Amy Mondloch in Chapter 8. At the end of the daylong event, we organized the participants into discussion groups based on the drafted chapters. We asked them to start considering strategies for dealing with the issues expressed in those chapters. At the end of the day, in reporting out the small-group discussion results, we heard a consistent refrain across all the groups that one of the first things needed was a set of "community standards" for service learning.

We then got to work organizing meetings and strategizing ways to amplify the community's voice in service learning. We started with the research findings—adding, specifying, and refining the recommendations that naturally derived from that research with the participation of about thirty community organizations. They gave us a limit of one page to work with initially, which we negotiated into a trifold brochure. They did not, however, limit our elaboration on that six-column brochure elsewhere. So this chapter is our attempt to suggest practices that can meet the community's standards (see Stoecker and Tryon, 2007). You will notice that the standards refer mostly to things that those of us in higher education institutions should do. Given the structural power imbalances between higher education institutions and community organizations, this is fitting. Higher education has set the agenda of service learning for too long. Professors have determined which students will perform service learning and what courses will support it. Institutional service learning offices have set the purpose of it. Students have chosen placements on the basis of what interests them. Institutional-based actors have created a variety of service learning manuals, but they have all been based on the perceptions, needs, and desires of those on the institutional side of the divide. All of these actors have, consequently, implied to community organizations what they should accept.

This project is a counterbalance to those messages, and these recommendations are developed from the voices on the other side of the divide. During the meetings that hammered out these standards, community organization representatives acknowledged that there are constraints on the faculty, administration, and resources of colleges and universities, and that they didn't expect all these recommendations to be consistently followed. However, they wanted to express their preferred methods of conducting service learning, with the goal of integrating more and more of them into common practice over time.

Some of these standards come directly from the preceding chapters, others extend what is in the chapters, and others are from new information that came to light through the six-month process of creating the brochure. The standards also prioritize the recommendations of the preceding chapters. However, you won't see everything that is in those chapters, because that would have taken more than one sheet of paper.

We had to choose the top recommendations and their subissues for this aspect of the project. Also, in contrast to Chapter 9, there are more concrete specifics here. We do not exactly provide a recipe, but we do provide what the community organizations say are the crucial ingredients. Those crucial ingredients organize into the five following categories:

- *Communication:* How and when should contact be initiated, what materials and vehicles are best for guiding the project, who should be responsible, and in what manner should communication be sustained throughout the project?
- *Developing Positive Relationships:* Time commitments, frameworks, ways of behaving, and respecting and clearly defining the expectations of the partnership in an ongoing fashion.
- *Providing an Infrastructure for Service Learning:* Offices of "community engagement" or service learning centers, and their value in helping define and implement projects and streamline access.
- *Managing Service Learners:* Including supervising, evaluating, and troubleshooting problems; deadlines, and ways of handling paperwork.
- *Promoting Diversity in Service Learning:* Developing a framework for cultural competency, including the student's self-reflection and identification; value of recruiting diverse pool of service learners.

The three Cs are spread throughout these categories. Because, ultimately, the three Cs are ineffective unless they occur in an integrated way. Communication without commitment and compatibility without communication, for example, will not lead to better service learning. In this chapter, then, we present the very concrete ways that the three Cs can be implemented in the most effective integrated way.

Communication

Communication is the most fundamental component of service learning that serves communities. Even before relationships, communication provides the glue that allows committed relationships to form and last. And it can't be taken for granted. Those in higher education institutions and those in community organizations exist to a certain extent in different cultures (Batenburg, 1995; Bacon, 2002). They use different words, do different things, and try to achieve different goals, so they need to explain just what it is they mean when using words like "syllabus" or "request for proposals" (RFP). Here are some basic guidelines for good communication:

Faculty

Call Ahead

Those faculty who are used to putting courses together at the last minute, or even later, will find these community standards most difficult to implement, for the first standard of communication is to communicate early. One of the most challenging aspects of service learning for community organizations is when a flock of students shows up on their doorstep hoping for an immediate service learning placement to meet a set of course requirements. As we have seen, the organizations try to be obliging and even take on students who don't fit their needs as a service to the student and the faculty—at a net loss for their own productivity. But a little advance communication can dramatically reduce the costs that community organizations have to bear, especially if the faculty expects an intensive service learning placement that lasts more than forty hours, or if they plan to send multiple students to an organization. Faculty preparing a course can generate a lot of goodwill by contacting potential placement organizations ahead of the course, asking if they are willing to take on students, how many they might accept, and the conditions under which they are willing to do so. Allowing organizations to say no, while reassuring them that they will be contacted with the next opportunity even if they refuse this time, will also produce a lot of goodwill.

Send a Syllabus

The second thing that organizations want from faculty is some knowledge of their expectations for the student's experience. Too often, students show up for a service learning placement, and community organization staff have no idea what is being expected of them. Students can, of course, bring a syllabus with them, but if the faculty are communicating with the organization staff anyway, they can help the organization to better prepare by sending a syllabus ahead of time. Better yet, they can show their commitment to achieving community goals by asking organizations for their input as they develop the syllabus. Faculty who want to impose a ten-hour service learning requirement on their students might learn, if they ask, that many community organizations find such required short-term service learning to be more of a burden than it is worth. They may also learn that community organizations can offer a lot of input into the course substance that can better prepare students for the service learning and even enhance what they learn from the experience. Collaborating with community organizations on syllabus development can also make service learning less of an add-on and more of an integrated feature of the syllabus. Fortunately, along with the wisdom that can be gained from community organization staff, there are also readily available syllabi across the Internet to use as a guide.

Invite the Organization to Class

This may seem like putting yet another burden on the community organization, but many of them very much enjoy coming to the classroom. As discussed in Chapter 3, many community organization staff do not find volunteer fairs all that useful, and see classrooms as places where they can communicate with students and consequently better recruit student volunteers. It is very important to reassure organizations that they will receive future offers regardless of whether they decline the current offer to visit a class. If the community organization representative is doing more than just pitching his or her own program, and is involved in teaching a class session, it is worth trying to find them at least a token honorarium to recognize their value. Setting up a class session with a nonprofit staff person also encourages the early communication that is so helpful for successful service learning. There are times when it is possible to take the class to the organization, meeting on their turf. One of the challenges we are seeing in service learning is the number of students who are reluctant to go far from campus to do their service learning (Stoecker, Stern, and Hathaway, 2007). Holding class on the community organization's turf can support students in venturing off-campus.

Organizations

Assess Your Capacity to Manage Service Learners

Many of our community organizations are fairly self-critical of their service to students. Remember, they take on students not purely, or in some cases even primarily, out of an expectation that the students will increase their productivity. Often, they believe in the mission of educating the student and hope for some future impact that may shift the student's career aspirations or social consciousness. Because of these altruistic motives, many organizations pay even less attention to their own capacity to take on service learners than they would if they were thinking only of their own self-interest. So the advice that organizations give to each other is to pay attention to what it takes to manage service learners. Not doing so can further undermine the organization's experience of service learning, and also the student's experience. Assessing the organization's capacity to take on service learners starts with knowing what the needs are and what staff time is available. It can be difficult to judge how much time it takes to set up and manage a service learning placement. Organizations with volunteer coordinators are often in a better position to make those judgments than organizations that add volunteer management onto an existing position.

Provide Welcome Packets and Guidelines

Having assessed its capacity for service learning, the organization will also know better what it wants from students and what it can provide to them. One of the recommendations organizations made to themselves for improving service learning is to produce welcome packets and guidelines for students. Doing so has some up-front costs; in the end, however, it can solve some of the recurring problems cited by organization staff. For the numerous students who show up knowing nothing about the organization, it can save making the same presentation innumerable times during the semester. It also provides, in writing, expectations that can allow students to judge whether the placement will be right for them, and can support organizations in holding students accountable for meeting those expectations. This is more general than a memorandum of understanding that establishes specific service learning project expectations, and may focus on things such as professional deportment and overall office operation, which can be helpful for all volunteers.

Offer to Give Class Presentations

The flip side of faculty inviting organization staff to classes is organizations suggesting and accepting that activity. Ideally, organizing a class presentation involves a fair amount of communication between the professor and the nonprofit organization representative. It presents an ideal opportunity to hand out information that explains the nonprofit's mission and programs and guidelines for service learners, and to make face-to-face contact with faculty and students.

Organizations and Faculty Together

Familiarize Students with the Organization's Programs and Mission

Certainly it is a good idea for organizations to provide welcome packets and give class presentations as a way to acquaint students with their work. But printing out all those packets and showing up for all those presentations is expensive and time consuming. Faculty can help out here by doing some of this work as well. If they plan on having students work with particular organizations (see "Call Ahead" above), they can assist in acquainting students with the group, using institutional resources to make handouts on the organization. This work will help students judge their compatibility with particular agencies. Given the gulf between the nonprofit world and academia, helping students to bridge the separate worlds of nonprofit work and higher education requires that organizations understand the kinds of things students need to have defined and that faculty understand what organizations want to communicate about themselves. That can only be done by good communication and collaboration.

Sign a Contract or Memorandum of Understanding

Probably the most important part of assuring good communication between the faculty, student, and organization staff is establishing some kind of written agreement between the three of them. The purpose is not just to promote accountability, but to support all the participants in going through the process of creating a good project plan and specifying everyone's part in that plan. Participants should include things in the agreement document like a definition of service learning, learning objectives, responsibilities, time commitment, timeline, supervision, training, evaluation, and liability/risk management issues (background checks, transportation, etc.). But it is the process that leads up to the document that is important, not the document itself. We are, consequently, somewhat skeptical of cookie-cutter contract templates and, in fact, prefer that collaborators use more of an abbreviated form of strategic planning to create custom-designed agreement documents (Stoecker, 2005; Lyddon, 1999; Alliance for Nonprofit Management, 2003–2004).

Developing Positive Relationships

Communication provides the foundation for service learning relationships that serve all the partners. But good communication is just a starting point. To achieve real commitment and compatibility in a service learning arrangement, there are also certain efficiencies and frameworks that need to be developed. It is possible, for example, to send a syllabus, call an organization ahead of time, and complete a memorandum of understanding without really serving the organization. And since truly honest communication is something that grows over time as trust develops, there are other relationship issues that need to be addressed from the beginning.

Faculty

Make as Long a Commitment as Possible
The shorter the commitment, the less useful it is for the organization. Many organizations want a commitment that runs multiple years, especially from faculty; most want a commitment that runs at least for a full semester. And unless the ten- to twenty-hour service learning projects are very carefully designed, they are often a net loss for community groups. Faculty and students should not expect organizations to provide short-term service learning students with anything more than superficial assignments like stuffing envelopes and setting up chairs for meetings, unless they have carefully worked out a project plan in advance or their agency is geared toward tasks that are in line with the students' skills coming in. If they want deeper experiences, they are going to have to make deeper commitments to the organization, or thoughtfully provide a project plan that the agency finds of value.

Clearly Define the Students' Requirements for the Organization

It is shocking how many organizations don't even know if the students working with them are from a service learning course, an internship or independent study, or just volunteers. If the professor has learning objectives that the students are supposed to meet, the organizations want to know what those are so that they can provide appropriate training and experiences. They can also advise the professor on whether such expectations are realistic within the constraints of the commitments the professor and student are making. Organizations are happy to help provide experiences to support students in meeting course requirements, provided that they get appropriate returns on their investment of time and energy, but they cannot offer the experiences if they don't know what the requirements are.

Help Agency Staff Mentor Service Learners

It is important for community agencies to have some institutional support in mentoring the students in their charge. Faculty too often send students out to do service learning expecting the organization staff to provide free training—effectively reducing the faculty's teaching time without providing any remuneration to the community organization staff who are picking up the slack. Faculty who have long-term relationships with community organizations can provide much of the mentoring themselves, reducing the burden on the organization and creating a stronger connection between the course material and the community experience.

Respect the Work of the Agency

As we have seen, too much service learning privileges student learning over actual community service. As such, whether intended or not, it communicates a fundamental disrespect of the communities and community organizations that host service learners. The community is not a "laboratory" to be manipulated and experimented upon, or where students can learn by making mistakes. Respecting the work of the agency means understanding that they are dealing with serious social issues that need reliable resources, realizing that the communities they work with have their own wisdom that needs to be part of the solution, and knowing that mistakes have real consequences. In practice, this means respecting staff time, for example, by not sending thirty students individually to an agency to find out what they do. It means respecting organizational priorities, and not sending students two weeks before the end of the semester, expecting them to be offered a ten-hour service learning placement. It means being aware that the organizational calendar, not the institutional calendar, is the basis for organizing the service learning. This will avoid problems like an after-school program that is suddenly without volunteers because the university semester ends a month before the regular school semester. Developing projects collaboratively with organization staff and communicating continuously with them during the course of the project are the most effective ways to implement a respect for their work.

"Globalize" Opportunities

If we shift service learning thinking from what faculty, students, and higher education institutions need to what communities and organizations need, one of the things we begin to look for is how to orient the work of the academy differently. While faculty are used to attending lots of meetings where very little happens, community organization staff don't have such luxury. They are not as willing, nor do they have the capacity, to attend six separate meetings with faculty who want to place service learning students, or serve on multiple "advisory groups" to multiple service learning efforts. Consequently, we need to look for efficiencies at the academy. Such strategies include combining or piggybacking on existing meetings. Faculty can attend organization board meetings or many professors can meet simultaneously with an organization. Faculty and students can even do group tours of a community site or group orientations. Such things take some coordination time by both faculty and organization staff (who are likely the only ones who will have a list of all the faculty trying to place students with them), but it is important not to expect organization staff to take sole responsibility for organizing these collective activities.

Protect Organization Choice

We have seen that the control of service learning by higher education institutions has created structures, such as volunteer fairs, that are not always very useful for community groups. Nevertheless, the organization staff still feel compelled to show up, even when they don't expect to get anything out of it, for fear that they will not receive other offers if they decline. Institutions need to explicitly tell organizations that they will not be removed from any list except by their choice, regardless of what they participate in or what criticisms they provide of institutional activities. To a large extent, this is something that should be addressed by institutional policy, but in the absence of such policy, individual faculty will need to provide these assurances.

Encourage Organizations to Be Selective

Similar to protecting organization choice, institutions need to support them in making sure service learning meets their needs, not just those of faculty and students. They should not take on students who have nothing to offer them or their communities. Faculty can support the organizations by explaining to students that they may have to apply and interview for service learning positions and can be rejected, so that they may have to try somewhere else where their skills are a better fit. Restricting access to service learning in such a way will also encourage the institution side to better prepare students to provide quality service.

Providing an Infrastructure

One of the most concrete ways to nurture the relationship between faculty and community organization staff is to provide professional resources to help create successful service learning experiences. If the institution is forward-looking, it probably already has or is now developing some type of "Center for Community Engagement" or other office of service learning. The people who staff these offices are a crucial link to the long-term success of service learning. Ideally, they are on the payroll to facilitate engagement activities and act as a liaison and technical assistance provider to parties both inside and outside the college or university. They can provide assistance in innumerable ways, helping to: develop projects, find matches between faculty and community organizations, facilitate communication, advocate for nonprofits, provide training, and troubleshoot placements. The community organizations' recommendations for community engagement and service learning offices cover these and other issues, showing how valuable this service can be to the university-community relationship.

Help Define "Service Learning"

Many of the community organizations we interviewed did not have a clear definition of service learning. Not all community organization staff are familiar with the language used in higher education to define service learning as a concept distinct from volunteering. The community engagement office can help present the office's mission statement and explain their definition of service learning, emphasizing the idea that students are receiving course credit for an engagement experience and thus certain learning objectives have been set. Based on what non-profit staff said about the students sent to them, we suspect many faculty don't have a good definition of service learning either, and may require the same service.

Streamline the Process of Finding Matches

There are always requests from community organizations for project support, and requests from faculty looking for service learning opportunities that fit specific academic criteria. If an office can keep tabs on both streams of information, it is easier to make connections that serve all parties. It is important, however, not to take the easy way out and just create a set of Web forms. Organization staff in particular value personal relationships, and the community engagement office should support such relationship building.

Create Databases

While it is important not to rely solely on electronic databases, it is still important to develop them. Such databases should include a list of professors who teach service learning classes or have community partnerships, opportunities posted by organizations that faculty and students can access, and a listing of organizations that accept service learners. These databases need to be constructed with the needs of their audiences in mind. In some areas, there are several institutions attempting to develop partnerships in the community. We heard a few times from community organization staff: "It's a pain to have to sign up and send updates to different places—we'd like to do it just once." Sadly, such interinstitutional coordination is still beyond the abilities of most higher education institutions, but if we really care about serving the community organizations, we will create regional clearinghouses where community organizations can input their information just once in a location where students from multiple institutions can access it. In addition, many databases are not structured to maximize communication to the most appropriate students. For example, a good database should allow a neighborhood center that needs help with its outreach and communications to word and target its request to be attractive to marketing majors, communication arts, or graphic design students, or to students with whatever particular combinations of skills that would be of most value.

Keep in Touch with Community Partners

In many ways, community engagement offices need to build relationships and maintain communication with both nonprofit staff and faculty to support the fragile communication chain between student, faculty, and agency, and maintain accountability for service learning projects. This often requires site visits or other face-to-face meetings. It can also add an additional communication burden on the organization, but most organization staff are receptive to an occasional follow-up call from a service learning office after students have been placed to make sure everything is going okay. When things are not going well, having a third party can help with sometimes emotionally challenging troubleshooting.

Run Orientations for Service Learners

To reduce the burden on organizations, and compensate for the understandable lack of faculty knowledge on how nonprofits operate, community engagement offices can organize and implement orientations on things like office etiquette, professional behavior, and cultural competence. As we heard from some agency staff, students sometimes arrive unprepared to "be in an office." And while agency staff do not expect them to live up to the exact standards they set for themselves, they do need students to be prepared to be productive participants in the office. Dress code, phone manners, interaction with staff members, and especially cultural competency are all areas where training can be developed and standardized at the institutional level through an office dedicated to community engagement.

Run Orientations for Organizations

While many nonprofit staff may have gotten their degrees at the same local higher education institution, accessing the institution as a community organization is very different from accessing it as a student. Thus, community engagement offices can also provide orientations for organization staff on how to access campus resources, and provide information about service learning in a user-friendly environment.

Provide Organizations with "Zero-Dollar Appointments"

Agency staff often justifiably feel that, when they are supervising service learners, they are essentially acting as their instructors—and, indeed, they are. Maybe they are not teaching out of a textbook, but they are providing an experiential education that is impossible to duplicate in the classroom. Even if we give them zero dollars for their work, it makes sense to give them the respect due to an instructor by offering them access to the institutional resources that are available to faculty, and which allow organization staff to better mentor students. Many organization staff need library access, others would like computer network access to various online resources and services only available to those with a user name and password, and others need parking benefits to facilitate meeting with faculty and students. Providing access to campus recreational and entertainment resources also symbolically recognizes the importance of the community mentor. Zero-dollar appointments can include all of these privileges.

Managing Service Learners

The pieces of managing, evaluating, and supervising service learners are critical to the success of a service learning project. Although there is overlap here with the section on communication and relationships, it bears repeating that work done at the beginning of the project will pay off many times over—just as laying a solid foundation for a building ensures that the walls and roof are straight. The following recommendations from our community organizations focus on the specific kinds of communication and relationship-building practices that are important once the project has commenced:

Organizations and Faculty Together

Determine the Organization's Role in Evaluation

The first step in assessing the student's performance in a service learning assignment is to agree on what role organization staff will play in the evaluation. We heard of significant variation in the evaluation of service learners. Some faculty have never evaluated student performance at the service learning site and consider the students' impact on the community to be unimportant. From a community perspective, that position is untenable. But there is also variation in how much organization staff want to be involved in evaluating students, so discussion with agency staff about their role in evaluation is very important. Some agencies don't know whether anything they say has any impact on the student's grade, so they would like to be consulted about the evaluation process up front. Knowing what is being asked of them also helps them judge their own capacity to take on service learners. It also allows the organization to give input into what methods of evaluation should be used.

Agree on the Criteria and Process That Will Be Used to Evaluate the Student

Even if organization staff don't want to be involved in the evaluation, they likely have some standards that students should meet, so most organizations would like to have a part in the control of this piece of the service learning experience. If the student does an outstanding job and the organization staff gives a glowing evaluation, it's nice for them to know that the work they put into writing it actually has some effect on the grade the student receives. By the same token, occasionally students will not take their service learning placement seriously or will do actual harm in the community, and the agency can get very frustrated if they have no vehicle to let the instructor know what did or did not happen.

Evaluate Midway and at the End of the Course and Use the Evaluations to Improve the Course

The midpoint is a good time to check in on the student's performance, so that the assignment can be tweaked and any problems that may have arisen can be worked out before it's too late. Sometimes this is as simple as a midterm phone call to check in, and sometimes it is more formal. Having a memorandum of understanding in place and an agreed-upon assessment process can also greatly facilitate the midterm evaluation, as all parties will know what goals are to be considered.

Limit Paperwork

If we keep in mind that service learning is not the organization's primary mission, and that real service is essential, we will come up with forms of managing and evaluating service learners that support quality work without unduly burdening organization staff. Consequently, a phone call interview or e-mail response may be easier than extensive forms: We heard that many organization staff were hard to reach and hard-pressed to return phone messages, so they preferred a quick e-mail asking a few pertinent questions. Others were happier talking by phone or even directly face-to-face than writing at all. The key is to find out what method they prefer when making the initial contact with the agency and setting up the parameters of the evaluation process.

Determine Who Grades or Checks that Hours and Duties Have Been Completed

Outside the issue of how to evaluate performance is basic service learning bookkeeping. This can go back to the contract or memorandum of understanding. An important component of that agreement is what role the organization will play in the student's grade. This can relate to overall grading if there is a percentage of the grade that is based on completing all the hours or showing up at certain times. Here, at least some of the burden must fall on the organization, as the instructor is likely not on-site at the agency. Simply tracking hours can also enhance communication.

Students

Commit to the Organization's Cause

Like faculty, students need to make the shift from thinking of service learning as serving the student to the student serving the community. This means making a commitment to the community and the organization beyond the course credit they will receive. The historical bias in service learning to student learning rather than community development has meant that students have not been asked to make serious commitments to communities. This is exacerbated by the practice of required service learning, as there is a limit on how much commitment the organization can realistically expect when instructors make service learning mandatory and give little or no choice of placement. When faculty place students at agencies in which they are genuinely interested, it naturally creates a situation where the experience will be richer and more productive for all parties involved. That is why it is so important for students to understand the organization they might be working with. The obvious examples of a bad fit include assigning a student opposed to contraception and abortion to Planned Parenthood, or the reverse, sending a pro-choice student into an agency that requires volunteers to sign a "pro-life" statement before they can have any contact with pregnant clients. But sending students to work with an antipoverty agency when the student believes that poverty is the result of laziness is also not appropriate. This means that students need to be clear about their own values and faculty need to help them make their values explicit. To make that process accountable, organizations need to feel safe screening students based on their values.

Be Self-Directed and Follow the Professional Etiquette of the Organization

It is most helpful to the organization if students have received an orientation to professional behavior in a nonprofit context, have the requisite social skills, and take to heart whatever directives they have been given regarding dress code, cell phone usage, communication style, and any other ground rules for "being in an office." Agencies would also like students to do their best to complete tasks without a lot of micromanagement, and pitch in when they see something they might be able to help with. Community agency staff do not see their office as a site primarily for students to learn these basic skills, and students should not be sent into the community primarily for that purpose.

Be Responsible for Their Institutional Requirements and Deadlines

This is part of the training in professional deportment. Organization staff don't want to be treated as glorified babysitters. If the instructor requires students to get their hours in by a certain time, organization staff expect students to meet their deadlines without burdening the organization. It shows an extreme lack of consideration when a student shows up at an agency two weeks before the term ends, as one did in this study, and says, "I need twenty hours by the end of this week!" By some odd stroke of luck, the agency might be able to put a student to work for such a large chunk of time right away, but if not, he or she is just deadweight.

Meeting such deadlines also often means working ahead with either a memorandum of understanding or an evaluation form. Remember, organization staff are there primarily for the community, not the student, and they should not be asked for a twenty-four-hour turnaround on an evaluation form just so the student can graduate. Organization staff need a reasonable amount of lead time to reflect on and complete such paperwork.

Adapt to the Organization's Scheduling and Program Framework

Everyone on the academic side of the service learning partnership, including the student, needs to understand that in order to truly serve the community, the community's calendar must take precedence. The needs of the agency don't necessarily stop over holidays, and in fact may even increase, especially at social service agencies like food pantries and crisis centers for family problems, domestic abuse, and the like. These things often don't fit neatly into a "normal" workweek, either. The more flexible the student is, the more likely he or she will have a positive service learning experience and be able to provide useful service. A student who is available at short notice, for example, may be allowed to shadow a staff member doing an intake on a family in crisis, as opposed to expecting those types of situations to occur only from 10:00 to noon on Tuesdays. If, as we hope, community agencies will become more selective about the service learners they take on, the students who show the greatest commitment and most serious accommodation to the organization's needs will have access to the most exciting and rewarding placements.

Keep the Lines of Communication Open with Faculty and Organization

While student learning has been the emphasis in service learning, the neglect of students' impact on the community has also hindered that learning. The lack of communication and relationship between faculty and organization has meant that the problems students encounter, and sometimes contribute to, often are not addressed until it is too late. We are hopeful that more faculty will begin to take a significant interest in community outcomes, with encouragement and better resources such as those discussed here. Students can help to facilitate communication in the meantime. Sometimes the student is the only one who knows all the pieces of information and all the parties involved. Communicating between the parties, including things like sharing information on course requirements and materials, as well as organization conflicts and trials, will help forestall difficulties or catch problems before they become too large.

Organizations

Complete Evaluations as Agreed Upon

It may go without saying that community organization staff might feel skeptical that their evaluations would be taken seriously. But turning the ship of service learning to point to community outcomes rather than primarily student outcomes actually requires agency staff to involve themselves in steering that ship. And that means taking advantages of the opportunities that do exist to evaluate both student performance and service learning program effectiveness. It's only fair that organizations make their best attempt to return paperwork or phone messages within the time frame that the faculty has asked. Obviously, if they don't return evaluations, the instructor can't use them to assign the grade. Unforeseen circumstances do arise, especially in the daily-crisis mode of much community agency life, and faculty need to understand short delays. If a homeless and hungry family has just shown up at the doorstep of a social service agency, of course that will take priority over paperwork, and faculty will probably be sympathetic to extending a deadline or working out another way to deliver the feedback.

Here again, a commitment to quality planning at the beginning of the project will make a final evaluation so much easier. And for those organizations concerned about being left out of future opportunities, it is not the organization that declines an opportunity that is most likely to be excluded from future offers, but the one that says yes and doesn't follow through.

Communicate Challenges or Problems with Students to Faculty in a Timely Fashion

If everyone has committed to and follows through on the standard of evaluating at both midterm and end-of-term time points, the vast majority of challenges that everyone encounters in service learning will be manageable. But there are also occasions when it is obvious at the beginning that a student is a bad fit, or that the planned project won't work out. If the professor doesn't know, he or she can't help fix the problem. And the fixes that the organization might propose could interfere with the professor's learning objectives. Additionally, the student is ultimately the responsibility of the professor, not the organization, and it is reasonable for agency staff, rather than taking complete responsibility for the student, to alert the instructor to communicate with the student and find out what's going on.

Promoting Diversity

In settings such as Madison, Wisconsin, this is the hardest of all the standards to meet. We have no good models or programs in place that promote diversity in service learning. And our veneer of progressivism makes it very difficult to surface veneer-dissolving issues like institutionalized racism. We suspect more-diverse communities may have less difficulty here, but even in those places, we have no ready models for designing service learning programs to draw on the strengths of diversity and repair the damage that has been done by hatred and forced inequality. Even our community organizations lack the diversity needed to fully address this problem, but they have made a start here.

Organizations and Faculty

Work Together to Develop Goals and Processes for Student Cultural Competency

The challenge of developing cultural competency, in our particular context, is that neither the nonprofit sector nor the higher education sector effectively operationalizes the diversity they are trying to educate students to appreciate. Achieving student cultural competency involves also attaining such competency among both faculty and organization staff and modeling diversity in both settings. We don't know what such a comprehensive program would look like, but it is clear that such a program is necessary.

Help Students Understand and Reflect on Social Status and Self-Identity

As discussed in Chapter 7, the path to developing cultural competency begins with understanding oneself. It is true that the majority of service learners are relatively privileged young white women, who our organizations noted to be particularly unskilled when it comes to crossing racial and ethnic boundaries. Some agency staff, however, noted that they had students from working-class backgrounds and minority racial-ethnic backgrounds who could also benefit from self-reflection on how structural dynamics of race, class, sex or gender, ability, and other social categories affect their lives. Ideally, understanding how diversity operates in the student's own life and in the community should occur before the student enters the field, as the student will often be working with people who could also benefit from reflecting on the role of socially structured diversity and the inequality that goes with it. When the student and community member do that together, they take the first step toward strategizing ways to struggle against social structural exclusion.

Provide Feedback on Student Cultural Competency, Including Student Reflection

Because it is so difficult to talk about oppression, much of the cultural-competency training tends to involve lectures and PowerPoint presentations. But cultural competency takes practice and coaching, and that can only be done through interaction. Hopefully, faculty can organize their service learning classrooms in such a way that students can feel safe developing and practicing their cultural-competency skills. If the community is not a place to send students to make mistakes, the classroom is the quintessential site for mistake making. This necessitates a transformation of the classroom process, however. Lectures will need to be replaced with discussions, role-playing, and journaling. Faculty will need to adopt a coaching model of teaching, where they give frequent and custom-designed personal feedback rather than just grading a midterm and a final (Palmer, 1998; Barr and Tagg, 1995). Organization staff can be brought into the classroom to participate and also to coach, allowing them to see the strengths and weaknesses of prospective service learners and begin to build relationships with those they would invite to their organization and community. They can then continue that coaching in the field. Thinking in this open, inclusive way about assets of the community and the institution together can create powerful new synergy.

Work Together with Students to Handle Cultural Conflicts as They Occur

If cultural-competency training begins in the classroom, involving organization staff and other community members when possible and where there are resources to support their involvement, there will already be relationships when students enter the field. When a student behaves insensitively, there may then be enough of a relationship to use the incident as a learning experience that strengthens rather than weakens the relationships. Liken this to any strong relationship—you don't ask someone about his or her personal life until you establish trust and rapport—there's no shortcut to skipping this step with campus-community partnerships.

Institutions

Actively Recruit More Diverse Students to Service Learning

Many of our community organizations emphasized that they need and value service learners of color who can be role models for members of communities of color. Providing such students is a tall order when so many higher education institutions have problems recruiting students of color in general. But here again, shifting the emphasis in service learning can help. Chapter 7 discusses that students of color are not enthusiastic about the charity model of service learning. That probably also means that they are not enthusiastic about the charity model of social service either, which is the dominant model practiced by nonprofit service learning hosts. Recruiting students of color to service learning, then, may require transforming the ways that both service learning and social services are delivered. It may also involve targeting service learning more toward social action and social justice organizations, at least some of which we have learned feel excluded from access to service learners. Institutions have historically shied away from supporting such organizations and the faculty who work with them, so this is a tall order to fill (Robinson, 2000, 2000b; Gedicks, 1996).

Provide Comprehensive Cultural-Competency Training

While the planning and development of cultural-competency training must come from faculty and community organization staff, its implementation must be supported by higher education institutions. Such training needs to be integrated into the curriculum, officially supported, and funded. Handling service learning correctly, in ways that truly impact communities, requires small classes and takes much more faculty time. If faculty are expected to develop cultural competency themselves and then coach students in it, institutions are going to have to commit far more resources to rebalance teaching loads. However, institutions should also provide training for larger groups of students across courses, such as campuswide seminars, rather than training classroom by classroom.

Students

Work to Understand Social Status, Self-Identity, and Community Strengths in Their Service Learning Site

Even the best cultural-competency training will have little impact, of course, if students do not engage themselves in the process. But asking the students to engage in a process of understanding self and other also means supporting them through the process. And, here again, the problem itself points to the wrongheadedness of current service learning models, especially the required service learning model. If service learning becomes a privilege for which students must apply and interview, one of the criteria for allowing students to undertake service learning can be their willingness to engage in self-reflective cultural-competency work. We must make such work as safe as possible, however, so that students will want to become culturally competent, and grow through it rather than shrink from it. Students certainly have a responsibility here, but only when faculty, organizations, and higher education institutions have put into place the necessary supports.

Actively Reflect on Their Experience and Share Those Reflections with Agency Staff

The community organizations expressed sincere hope and interest in learning what the students' reactions to the environment were after their assignments were over. And why wouldn't they be interested? The feedback from a fresh perspective could, in some cases, be very valuable in assessing an agency's programs and mode of interaction with clients and students. If we are successful in transforming service learning from within higher education institutions, we will have created the infrastructure upon which students can grow to the benefit of their service learning sites rather than at the expense of their host communities.

Conclusion: Toward Service Learning that Serves Everyone

Through working with dozens of community organizations over just the last year and a half, we have had our eyes opened. We have seen how the traditional models of service learning that emphasize required, short-term placements of poorly prepared students doing charity work with little to no communication between agency and institution and with absent faculty, can be less than useful to the community. We are amazed at the willingness of community organizations to take on such service learners as an additional mission, in the hopes that they will be able to impact student attitudes, at significant cost to their own productivity and with no remuneration.

Such a model is unsustainable in the long term. Community impact must be at least as important as student impact. Faculty engagement is a necessity, not an option. Service learning office structure and function needs to be rethought in view of these findings. Institutional rewards must be reprioritized.

We are aware that what we found in our context may not apply in others. We would like to stress that there are many sensitive faculty who "get it" and are engaged with their service learning sites. We work with many who want to handle service learning correctly and are eager to listen to what we've found out and follow it as closely as possible for their class projects. There are service learning offices that are doing their best to prepare students. There are service learning programs that emphasize community impact. But as yet, we do not have a compendium of promising practices that can guide the ship of service learning away from the rocks.

The starting point, we believe, is to attend to the unheard voices—the staff of community organizations and the members of their host communities, who have been suffering through neglectful models of service learning for too long. Our humble offering for the time being is this list of recommendations from them to you, the reader. There is one caveat: We don't just want the community standards created by the organizations in our community to become a boilerplate substitute for the process of hearing the voices of those in other communities. It's going to work best when each community makes it a priority to amplify the unheard voice in every site where service learning is practiced, and for each community to develop its own standards for service learning. We hope that others find our process more important than our product, for it is the process that builds the relationships needed to design service learning that serves everyone.

The agency staff whose voices you have heard in this volume hope the standards they have created with us will be taken up by our local faculty and administrators and used to help prepare and implement better service learning projects. It is a living document: Since the main presence is Web-based, it can be constantly revised and printed in small quantities so it stays current (as opposed to spending a bundle to print a thousand copies on slick, expensive, glossy magazine stock). The organizations also wanted us to stress that they understand not all the standards can realistically be applied to each and every instance of service learning practice. They are aware that "life happens" and do not by any means intend to sound absolutist about accepting students into their organizations based on whether faculty and institutions can deliver each standard to their strict specifications. But they do want us to try.

Epilogue: The Two Futures of Service Learning

RANDY STOECKER AND ELIZABETH TRYON

O ne of the definitions of an epilogue is a speech at the end of a literary work that deals with the future of its characters. Such a definition is fitting for this concluding chapter. Our cast of major characters—students, faculty, service learning administrators and staff, and particularly community organization staff—is actually part of a story whose next chapter could follow two very different timelines. One timeline engages our cast in service learning as it is currently practiced, with not enough attention to community outcomes or the institutional changes needed to make those outcomes useful. The alternate timeline engages our cast in a very different form of service learning where community outcomes are the first priority, not the last, and service learning is structured to maximize community impact.

Which timeline will win out? We don't know. As we have presented this research at conferences and campuses, and sent papers to journals, we have received three reactions. The first reaction has come from nonprofit staff, whose animated nods are followed by hallway conversations that relay yet another story of service learning-as-usual making their lives difficult. In one of these cases, the story actually came from a faculty member at one of the local higher education institutions who was also a board member of a nonprofit organization that works with handicapped individuals. She related her disappointment and resentment that the service learning project she was involved in had fallen flat. Her nonprofit was looking for someone to design a Web portal for potential clients, and was assured by an eager faculty member that a computer skills class could do something simple in one semester. Trusting in the process, she placed the responsibility in the hands of the class. Not only was the project never delivered, but after numerous phone calls to the professor, who promised to finish the Web site himself but then didn't, the nonprofit had to hire a professional at a considerable cost to do a rush job and get the site online in time for their spring registration deadline. She evinced the opinion that she will never again rely on students to produce anything of such importance to the organization. Instead, she will just give them "busy work" if they are sent to her in the future, no matter how tempting it might be to save the cash resources needed to have the work done professionally.

The second reaction has come from those academic-based service learning proponents who are so unable to accept the possibility that their form of service learning may be doing harm that they walk out on presentations, or express their denial from the shadows through anonymous reviews of journal articles. We have been surprised at the intensity of some of these reactions, which refer to our community organization staff as "a disgruntled minority," express offense at a critique of John Dewey, or respond that community organizations are simply going to need to adapt to the realities of higher education. These are the critics who will point to the superficial satisfaction surveys that show how grateful community organization hosts are for their service learners. It is exactly those satisfaction surveys, however, that illustrate just how much at arm's length so many academics hold their community organization hosts. The question is not whether community organization staff are superficially satisfied, but what they would change if given the opportunity to speak up and be heard. We didn't invite our agency partners to tell us how great we were, but how we could be better. It is in asking how we can do better that we begin the process of developing the strong relationships necessary for the best service learning.

The third reaction, thankfully more common than the second, has come from those academic-based service learning proponents who engage the issues this research raises, and are already searching for alternatives. Randy Stoecker recently organized a day-long workshop devoted exclusively to the question of how to maximize the community impact of service learning, attended by forty people—three-quarters of them academics. The academics, nearly all from Wisconsin with a small contingent from Iowa, worked tirelessly all day, and practiced their listening skills with the community organization staff in attendance. The group's recommendations appear on the project Web site (Stoecker and Schmidt, 2008b).

We can consequently see the dialectic starting to emerge as outright conflict. More and more community organization staff are becoming increasingly vocal about the shortcomings of service learning. Native communities in particular are refusing to be exploited by academics, by establishing their own institutional review processes and agreements that prevent the unwilling extraction of knowledge from their communities (Government of Canada, 2005). More academics are documenting those shortcomings. And the reactions of those who resist the reality that service learning is imperfect are becoming more intense. So we sense a storm brewing, and we are glad for it. The storm will not only bring with it the winds of change, but the rains to wash away the residue that has built up on the old service learning status quo and nourish the seedlings of new forms of higher education and community partnership to grow stronger communities.

We already have a sense of some of these new seedlings, in the form of project-based service learning and community-based research (CBR), both of which we have explored briefly in this work. Clearly, the CBR project that led to this book is also propelling the critique of service learning, in an infinite-mirror type of reflection. But can CBR by itself pave the way to the alternative? The strength of CBR is that it focuses everyone's efforts on completing an actual project. Three elements are needed in order for the project to be effective, even at a baseline level. Community organization staff need to know what they want the research to do. Faculty need to assure that the research will do what community organization staff want. Students need to effectively carry out the research. But if the CBR project is driven and steered from the academic side of the relationship, as is so often the case, it will be no better than service learning.

The challenge, we believe, is for CBR to make every effort to distinguish itself from service learning. And, at this point, we go further than even the recommendations of the community voices contained in this volume. In our view, too much CBR is biased toward academic rather than community interests. Instead, we need to develop service learning and CBR from a community development model (Stoecker, 2005). Such a model engages a process of organizing a community—not just its service providers but also its people—to define an issue. The issue can be the lack of places for kids to play, an absence of decent jobs, an excess of crime, or any other issue that the people of the community want to tackle. To address the issue effectively, it must be deeply understood—or diagnosed—by everyone involved. Doing that requires gathering information and engaging students, faculty, service providers, and residents in codesigning and carrying out the process. And then, of course, there must be a strategy—or prescription—for dealing with that issue. Developing a truly effective strategy also requires thoughtful consideration of the community context and the array of options, and carefully comparing each option to the context. Here again, an alliance of faculty, students, service providers, and residents can be a powerful change agent indeed.

This, of course, will help put the project into motion—the implementation. At this stage, we can practice something that looks more like typical service learning. The difference is that, rather than superficial make-work, now the service is part of a larger project, well-informed by thorough diagnostic and prescription processes and designed to tackle a community-defined issue. There are even more roles for everyone in evaluating whether the project is having the desired impacts, ending the historical neglect of the question of community impact.

Such a model, however, does not mesh with higher education as we know it. A community development process cannot operate on a semester or quarter system; it requires an ongoing long-term commitment and it necessitates the intimate engagement of higher education faculty and staff. That is a tall order, given what our research has shown about the current state of service learning. The ideal will not be achieved through a tweak here and an adjustment there. But the payoff can be rich indeed, if we do the advance preparation to ensure that engagement involves community input from the get-go. Learning will be more authentic because it will reflect what's really going on in the community in real time. The student objectives will be met at a deeper level and students will be better prepared to go out into the world with real-world problem-solving skills.

As the housing bubble bursts, the economy declines, energy prices see-saw, the climate changes, and global conflict seems as intractable as ever, perhaps we can begin to feel a bit more urgency than in days past, perhaps to the point where people in both the community and the academy will work more diligently to negotiate differences in language and culture and implement such a community development approach. If institutions of higher education do their best to work together with the communities that support them with students and other assets, they will be setting the example that society needs. It will take legions of ethical thinkers and actors to help human society step away from the brink of irreversible damage to the earth's environment, stop waging war and other injustices on each other, and get to the business of regeneration and social justice with our eye toward those who will come seven generations after us—the time-honored standard of future thinking promoted by Native American leaders such as Oren Lyons (1991). Even if service learning is regarded at its highest level as only a piece of that puzzle, it deserves to be done in good faith and as intelligently as possible to help create, first and foremost, powerful communities and college graduates that are thoughtful and informed world citizens who already have had some experience with community work. This may seem like a lofty goal, but there's no harm in striving for it and its myriad benefits, even if we only attain it in part.

So, which future are we capable of creating—service learning that is still driven mainly by the academy's wishes, or service learning that transforms all of which it is a part? The worst possible outcome would be for faculty, students, and service learning administrators to read these findings and decide to stop partnering with the smallest and most grassroots organizations, worried that they can't meet the standards described in these chapters. But that is a real risk. Higher education institutions, even though they try to operate as sites of knowledge innovation, are still beset by amazingly intense inertia. And their members—students, faculty, and administration—seem at times to be resist to change; sometimes for good reason, given the distrust that often exists between these groups. It would be a lot easier for those who control access to service learning to only serve the safe sites that don't ask for changes in the university calendar, for better preparation of students, or for increased commitment of faculty.

But now that community organizations are raising their voices through works such as ours, it may be too difficult to pull back. Already we are hearing from activist groups who believe they have long been unfairly denied access to higher education resources and services. And it is important to remember that, even though service learning may result in a net loss of productivity for many small- and medium-size nonprofits, and the current practice is far from the ideal that organization staff can imagine, they all are ready to keep trying to improve it.

We don't see any magic bullets that will bring about instantaneous reform, but hope that our project, along with other new research emerging, will be a small part of motivating the hard work to shift the balance of power to a more community-involved practice of community engagement by colleges and universities.

References

Adrian, J. Personal conversation with Elizabeth Tryon, May 2008, Madison, Wisconsin.

Allen, C. 2002. *Cultural Competency Training Template: An outline for a half-day program*. San Francisco, CA: Regents of the University of California. www.futurehealth.ucsf/pdf.files/Halfdaytemplate-network.pdf (accessed March 23, 2009).

Alliance for Nonprofit Management. 2003–2004. *Strategic planning*. www.allianceonline.org/FAQ/strategic_planning (accessed August 3, 2008).

Appreciative Inquiry Commons. 2007. http://appreciativeinquiry.case.edu/ (accessed August 3, 2008).

Bacon, N. 2002. Differences in faculty and community partners' theories of learning. *Michigan Journal of Community Service Learning* 9 (1): 34–44.

Barr, R. B., and J. Tagg. 1995. A new paradigm for undergraduate education. *Change*, November/December, 13–25.

Batenburg, M. P. 1995. Community agency and school collaboration: Going in with your eyes open. Paper presented at the annual meeting of the American Educational Research Association, San Francisco.

Bender, T. 1993. *Intellect and public life*. Baltimore, MD: Johns Hopkins University Press.

Benson, J. K. 1977. Organizations: A dialectical view. *Administrative Science Quarterly* 22 (1): 1–13.

———. 1983. A dialectical method for the study of organizations. In *Beyond method: Strategies for social research*, ed. G. Morgan, 331–46. Beverly Hills: Sage.

Benz, M. 2005. Not for the profit, but for the satisfaction? Evidence on worker well-being in non-profit firms. *Kyklos* 58 (2): 155–76.

Billig, S., S. Root, and D. Jesse. 2005. The relationship between the quality indicators of service-learning and student outcomes: Testing professional wisdom. In *Improving service-learning practice: Research on models to enhance impacts*, ed. S. Root, J. Callahan, and S. H. Billig, 97–118. Greenwich, CT: Information Age.

Birdsall, J. T. 2005. *Community voice: Community partners reflect on service learning.* www.mc.maricopa.edu/other/engagement/Journal/Issue5/Birdsall.pdf (accessed August 3, 2008).

Boise State University. 2005. *Agency handbook: Service-learning.* Boise, ID: Boise State University. http://servicelearning.boisestate.edu/upload/4/files/AGENCY%20HANDBOOK%20revised%201108.doc (accessed March 23, 2009).

Boyer, E. 1996. The scholarship of engagement. *Journal of Public Outreach* 1 (1): 11–20.

Bradford, M. 2005. Motivating students through project-based service learning. *THE Journal (Technological Horizons in Education)* 32 (6). http://thejournal.com/articles/17124 (accessed August 3, 2008).

Bringle, R. G., and J. A. Hatcher. 1996. Implementing service learning in higher education. *Journal of Higher Education* 67 (2): 221–40.

———. 1999. Reflection in service-learning: Making meaning of experience. *Educational Horizons* 77 (4): 179–85.

———. 2002. Campus-community partnerships: The terms of engagement. *Journal of Social Issues* 58 (3): 503–16.

Brown, D. M. 2001. *Putting it together: A method for developing service-learning and community partnerships based in critical pedagogy.* Washington, DC: Corporation for National Service. www.nationalservicere sources.org/filemanager/download/720/brown.pdf (accessed August 3, 2008).

Buhrmester, D., W. Furman, M. T. Wittenberg, and H. T. Reis. 1988. Five domains of interpersonal competence in peer relations. *Journal of Personality and Social Psychology* 55 (6): 991–1008.

Bushouse, B. K. 2005. Community nonprofit organizations and service-learning: Resource constraints to building partnerships with universities *Michigan Journal of Community Service Learning* 12 (1): 32–40.

Campus Compact. 2003. *Introduction to service learning toolkit: Readings and resources for faculty.* Providence, RI: Campus Compact.

Chamberlain, C. 2003. Teaching teamwork: Project-based service-learning course LINCs students with nonprofits. *Inside Illinois*, January 23. www .news.uiuc.edu/II/03/0123/linc.html (accessed August 3, 2008).

Cooperrider, D. L., and S. Srivastva. 1987. Appreciative inquiry in organizational life. *Research in Organizational Change and Development* 1: 129–69.

Coyle, E. J., L. H. Jamieson, and W. C. Oakes. 2005. EPICS: Engineering projects in community service. *International Journal of Engineering Education* 21 (1): 139–50. http://epics.ecn.purdue.edu/about/papers/ IJEE-0205.pdf (accessed August 3, 2008).

Cress, C. M., P. J. Collier, V. L. Reitenauer, and associates. 2005. Learning through serving: A student guidebook for service-learning across the disciplines. Sterling, VA: Stylus.

Cruz, N., and D. Giles. 2000. Where's the community in service-learning research? Special issue, *Michigan Journal of Community Service Learning* 7: 28–34.

Cutforth, N. J. 1999. Presentation at Bonner Community Research Project Gathering, Morehouse College, Atlanta.

Cutforth, N. J., and V. B. Stocking. 2005. Managing the challenges of teaching community-based research courses. Paper presented at the 5th Annual International Service Learning Research Conference, Michigan State University, East Lansing.

Daynes, G., and N. Longo. 2004. Jane Addams and the origins of service-learning practice in the United States. *Michigan Journal of Community Service Learning* 10 (3): 5–13.

Draper, A. J. 2004. Integrating project-based service-learning into an advanced environmental chemistry course. *Journal of Chemical Education* 81 (2): 221–24.

Driscoll, A., B. A. Holland, S. Gelmon, and S. Kerrigan. 1996. An assessment model for service-learning: Comprehensive case studies of impact on faculty, students, community, and institutions. *Michigan Journal of Community Service Learning* 3: 66–71.

Eby, J. 1998. *Why service-learning is bad.* http://sa-serenity.sa.utah.edu/ bennion/welch/wrongsvc.pdf (accessed August 3, 2008).

Ender, M., L. Martin, D. A. Cotter, B. M. Kowalewski, and J. DeFiore. 2000. Given an opportunity to reach out: Heterogeneous participation in optional service-learning projects. *Teaching Sociology* 28 (3): 206–19.

ERIC Development Team. 2001. Latinos in school: Some facts and findings (ED449288 2001-02-00). *ERIC Digest* 162. New York: ERIC Clearinghouse on Urban Education. www.eric.ed.gov/ERICDocs/data/ericdoc s2sql/content_storage_01/0000019b/80/16/cd/e0.pdf (accessed August 3, 2008).

Evans, S. M., and H. C. Boyte. 1992. *Free spaces: The sources of democratic change in America.* Chicago: University of Chicago Press.

Everyday Democracy (formerly the Study Circles Resource Center). 2005. "Everyday democracy: ideas and tools for community change." www .everyday-democracy.org/en/Index.aspx (accessed August 3, 2008).

Eyler, J., and D. E. Giles Jr. 1999. *Where's the learning in service-learning?* San Francisco: Jossey-Bass.

Ferrari, J. R., and L. Worrall. 2000. Assessments by community agencies: How "the other side" sees service-learning. *Michigan Journal of Community Service Learning* 7: 35–40.

Fiske, E. B. 2001. *Learning in deed: The power of service-learning for American schools.* Battle Creek, MI: W. K. Kellogg Foundation.

Fitch, P. 2005. In their own voices: A mixed methods approach to studying outcomes of intercultural service-learning with college students. In *Improving service-learning practice: Research on models to enhance impacts,* ed. S. Root, J. Callahan, and S. H. Billig, 187–214. Greenwich, CT: Information Age.

Fond du Lac Diversity Circles. n.d. www.fdl.uwc.edu/diversitycircles/index .html (accessed August 3, 2008).

Freire, P. 1985. *The politics of education: Culture, power, and liberation.* South Hadley, MA: Bergin and Garvey.

Gazley, B., and J. L. Brudney. 2005. Volunteer involvement in local government after September 11: The continuing question of capacity. *Public Administration Review* 65 (2): 131–42 (shortcomings of volunteers).

Gedicks, A. 1996. Activist sociology: Personal reflections. *Sociological Imagination* 33 (1) : 55–72. http://comm-org.wisc.edu/si/sihome.htm (accessed August 3, 2008).

Gelmon, S. B. 2003. Assessment as a means of building service-learning partnerships. In *Building partnerships for service learning,* ed. B. Jacoby, 42–64. San Francisco: Jossey-Bass.

Glaser, B. G., and A. L. Straus. 1967. *The discovery of grounded theory: Strategies for qualitative research.* New York: Aldine.

Gonzalez, J. 2007. *Links to service learning contract templates.* http://comm-org.wisc.edu/sl/page.php?2 (accessed August 3, 2008).

Gore, M. 2007. Sustaining a shared social space with a community services agency. Presentation at the American Democracy Project Conference, University of Wisconsin-River Falls.

Government of Canada. 2005. Tri-Council Policy Statement (TCPS): Section 6. Research involving aboriginal peoples. www.pre.ethics.gc.ca/english/policystatement/section6.cfm (accessed August 3, 2008).

Gugerty, C. R., and E. D. Swezey. 1996. Developing campus-community relationships. In *Service-learning in higher education: Concepts and practices,* ed. B. Jacoby et al. San Francisco: Jossey-Bass, 92–108.

Hall, K. 2006. Trent Centre for community-based education and the U-Links Centre for Community-Based Research. Public presentation, University of Wisconsin-Madison.

Holladay, J. 2006. Multicultural service-learning: Teacher planning sheet. Montgomery, AL: Southern Poverty Law Center. www.tolerance.org/teach/activities/activity.jsp?cid=729&ttnewsletter=torgnewsgen-062007 (accessed August 3, 2008).

Honnet, E. P., and S. Poulsen. 1989. *Principles of good practice for combining service and learning: A Wingspread special report.* Racine, WI: Johnson Foundation.

Hutchison, P. 2001. *Service learning: Challenges and opportunities.* www.newfoundations.com/OrgTheory/Hutchinson721.html (accessed August 3, 2008).

Jacoby, B. 1996. *Service-learning in higher education.* San Francisco: Jossey-Bass.

Jacoby, B., et al., eds. 2003. *Building partnerships for service learning.* San Francisco: Jossey-Bass.

Joint Educational Project. n.d. Service learning. www.usc.edu/dept/LAS/jep/sl/define_model.htm (accessed August 3, 2008).

Jones, S. R. 2003. Principles and profiles of exemplary partnerships with community agencies. In *Building partnerships for service learning,* ed. B. Jacoby et al., 151–73. San Francisco: Jossey-Bass.

Kahne, J., and J. Westheimer. 1996. In the service of what? The politics of service learning. *Phi Delta Kappan* 77 (9): 592–99.

Kaye, C. B. 2004. *The complete guide to service learning.* Minneapolis: Free Spirit.

Kellogg Commission. 1999. Returning to our roots: The engaged institution. www.nasulgc.org/NetCommunity/Document.Doc?id=183 (accessed August 6, 2008).

Kraft, R.J., and M. Swadener. 1994. *Building community: Service learning in the academic disciplines.* Denver: Colorado Campus Compact.

Krain, M., and A. M. Nurse. 2004. Teaching human rights through service learning. *Human Rights Quarterly* 26 (1): 189–207.

Lansverk, M. D. L. 2004. An apologie for service learning. *Montana Professor* 14 (2). http://mtprof.msun.edu/spr2004/lansverk.html (accessed August 3, 2008).

Lyddon, J. W. 1999. *Strategic planning in smaller nonprofit organizations: A practical guide for the process.* Kalamazoo: Western Michigan University. www.wmich.edu/nonprofit/Guide/guide7.htm (accessed August 3, 2008).

Lynch, R., and S. McCurley. 1999. Essential volunteer management. Seattle, WA: National CASA Association. www.casanet.org/program-management/volunteer-manage/essenvol.htm (accessed August 3, 2008).

Lyons, O. 1991. Oren Lyons the Faithkeeper. Interview by Bill Moyers. *Public Affairs Television,* July 3. www-tc.pbs.org/moyers/faithandreason/print/pdfs/faithkeeper.pdf (accessed August 3, 2008).

MacGregor, J., ed. 2003. *Integrating learning communities with service learning.* National Learning Communities Project Monograph Series. Olympia, WA: Evergreen State College with the American Association for Higher Education.

Manahan, R. A. 1980. Town and gown: The relationship between city and campus. *Vital Speeches of the Day* 46 (23): 717–21.

Marullo, S. 1998. Bringing home diversity: A service-learning approach to teaching race and ethnic relations. *Teaching Sociology* 26 (4): 259–75.

Marullo, S., and B. Edwards. 2000. From charity to justice: The potential of university-community collaboration for social change. *American Behavioral Scientist* 43 (5): 895–912.

Mays, N., and C. Pope. 2000. Assessing quality in qualitative research. *BMJ (British Medical Journal)* 320 (7226): 50–52. http://bmj.bmjjournals.com/cgi/content/full/320/7226/50?ijkey=3bdccabe44de53f59e50c7d9e61108d97aae4c69&keytype2=tf_ipsecsha (accessed August 3, 2008).

McCarthy, M. D. 1996. One-time and short-term service-learning experiences. In *Service learning in higher education: Concepts and practices*, ed. B. Jacoby et al., 113–34. San Francisco: Jossey-Bass.

McCurley, S. and R. Lynch. 1989. *Essential volunteer management*. Downers Grove, IL: VM Systems and Heritage Arts Publishing.

Metz, J., and J. Youniss. 2003. A demonstration that school-based required service does not deter, but heightens, volunteerism. *PS: Political Science & Politics* 36 (2): 281–86.

Mihalynuk, T. V., and S. D. Seifer. 2008. *Partnerships for higher education service-learning*. www.servicelearning.org/filemanager/download/two-page_fs/Partnerships_for_HE_SL_FS_Short_FINAL_Mar08.pdf (accessed August 3, 2008).

Mills, C. W. [1959] 1976. *The sociological imagination*. New York: Oxford University Press.

Mitchell, E. 2007. Cultural competency. Presentation at the State Superintendent and Wisconsin Campus Compact's PK-16 Institute for Service-Learning and Citizenship, Madison.

Mooney, L. A., and B. Edwards. 2001. Experiential learning in sociology: Service learning and other community-based learning initiatives. *Teaching Sociology* 29 (2): 181–94.

Morse, J. M., M. Barrett, M. Mayan, K. Olson, and J. Spiers. 2002. Verification strategies for establishing reliability and validity in qualitative research. *International Journal of Qualitative Methods* 1 (2): 13–22. http://ejournals.library.ualberta.ca/index.php/IJQM/article/view/4603/3756 (accessed August 3, 2008).

Morton, K. 1995. The irony of service: Charity, project and social change in service-learning. *Michigan Journal of Community Service-Learning* 2: 19–32.

Myers-Lipton, S. 1998. Effect of a comprehensive service-learning program on college students' civic responsibility. *Teaching Sociology* 26 (4): 243–58.

Network for Good. 2007. Volunteers. www.networkforgood.org/Npo/volunteers/default.aspx (accessed August 3, 2008).

Noley, S. 1977. Service-learning from the agency's perspective. *New Directions for Higher Education No. 18* 5 (2): 87–92.

Northland Poster Collective. 2006. If you have come to help me . . . http://northlandposter.com/blog/2006/12/18/lila-watson-if-you-have-come-to-help-me-you-are-wasting-your-time-but-if-you-have-come-because-your-liberation-is-bound-up-with-mine-then-let-us-work-together/ (accessed August 3, 2008).

Palmer, P. J. 1998. *The courage to teach.* San Francisco: Jossey-Bass.

Parker-Gwin, R., and J. B. Mabry. 1998. Service learning as pedagogy and civic education: Comparing outcomes for three models. *Teaching Sociology* 26 (4): 276–91.

Peacock, J. R., D. B. Bradley, and D. Shenk. 2001. Incorporating field sites into service-learning as collaborative partners. *Educational Gerontology* 27 (1): 23–35.

Pigza, J. M., and M. L. Troppe. 2003. Developing an infrastructure for service-learning and community engagement. In *Building partnerships for service learning,* ed. B. Jacoby et al., 106–30. San Francisco: Jossey-Bass.

Pribbenow, D. A. 2002. Exploring the impact of innovative pedagogy on faculty work: The case of service learning. PhD diss. University of Wisconsin.

Reed, V. A., G. C. Jernstedt, J. K. Hawley, E. S. Reber, and C. A. DuBois. 2005. Effects of a small-scale, very short-term service-learning experience on college students. *Journal of Adolescence* 28 (3): 359–68.

Rhoads, R. A. 1997. *Community service and higher learning: Exploration of the caring self.* Albany: State University of New York.

Robinson, T. 2000. Service learning as justice advocacy: Can political scientists do politics? *Political Science and Politics* 33 (3): 605–12.

———. 2000b. Dare the school build a new social order? *Michigan Journal of Community Service Learning* 7: 142–57.

Sandy, M., and B. A. Holland. 2006. Different worlds and common ground: Community partner perspectives on campus-community partnerships. *Michigan Journal of Community Service Learning* 13 (1): 30–43.

Scheibel, J., E. M. Bowley, and S. Jones. 2005. *The Promise of Partnerships: Tapping into the College as a Community Asset.* Providence, RI: Campus Compact.

Shaffett, B.R.D. 2002. Community organization staff perceptions about the importance of selected practices in building effective community-university service and learning partnerships. PhD diss., Louisiana State University. http://etd.lsu.edu/docs/available/etd-1113102-162549/ (accessed August 3, 2008).

Sherman, F. T., and W. R. Torbert, eds. 2000. *Transforming social inquiry, transforming social action: New paradigms for crossing the theory/practice divide in universities and communities.* Boston: Kluwer Academic.

Sigmon, R., N. Hemesath, and G. A. Witte. 1996. Evaluating a new service-learning program. In *Journey to service learning: Experiences from independent liberal arts colleges and universities*, ed. R. L. Sigmon and S. G. Pelletier. Washington, DC: Council of Independent Colleges.

Simmons, V. C., and P. Toole. 2003. *Service-learning diversity/equity project.* www.nylc.org/rc_downloaddetail.cfm?emoid=14:106 (accessed August 3, 2008).

Smith, L. T. 1999. *Decolonizing methodologies: Research and indigenous peoples.* New York: Zed Books.

Stoecker, R. 2005. *Research methods for community change: A project-based approach.* Thousand Oaks, CA: Sage Publications.

———. 2006. Dating to marriage: The opportunities and challenges of long-term university commitment to community. Keynote address, U-Links Celebration of Research, Haliburton, Ontario, Canada.

———. 2008. Challenging institutional barriers to community-based research. *Action Research* 6 (1): 49–67.

Stoecker, R., and C. Schmidt. 2008. Access to higher education service learning in rural areas. Paper presented at the Rural Sociological Society Annual Meetings, Manchester, Vermont.

———. 2008b. For Community's Sake: Maximizing the Community Impact of Service Learning. Conference Report, University of Wisconsin. http://comm-org.wisc.edu/sl/page.php?12 (accessed August 3, 2008).

Stoecker, R., E. Stern, and P. Hathaway. 2007. Managing service learners through a student intermediary and a project-based service learning model. Unpublished manuscript.

Stoecker, R., and E. Tryon. 2007. *Community standards for service learning.* http://comm-org.wisc.edu/sl/e107_files/public/cs4slbrochure.pdf (accessed August 3, 2008).

———. 2008. *The community side of service learning.* http://comm-org.wisc.edu/sl (accessed August 3, 2008).

Strand, K., N. Cutforth, R. Stoecker, S. Marullo, and P. Donohue. 2003. *Community-based research in higher education: Principles and practices.* San Francisco: Jossey-Bass.

Tiamiyu, M. F., and L. Bailey. 2001. Human services for the elderly and the role of university-community collaboration: Perceptions of human service agency workers. *Educational Gerontology* 27 (6): 479–92.

Tierney, W. G., and L. S. Hagedorn, eds. 2002. Increasing access to college: Extending possibilities for all students. Albany: State University of New York Press.

Timberlake, B. 2006. Personal communication with Elizabeth Tryon. Institute for Urban Life, Service Learning Program, Marquette University, Milwaukee, Wisconsin.

United Way's Latino Advisory Delegation. 2006. *Cuentamé: Latino Life in Dane County.* Madison, WI: United Way of Dane County. www.unitedwaydanecounty.org/pubs/LADReport.pdf (accessed August 3, 2008).

Valenciano, M. 2007. Cultural competency in the classroom. Keynote address, State of Oregon Training Summit, Salem. http://egov.oregon.gov/DAS/HR/docs/train/summit/Miguel.pdf (accessed August 3, 2008).

Vanderbilt University. 2008. *Guide on service-learning*. Nashville, TN: Center for Teaching. www.vanderbilt.edu/cft/resources/teaching_resources/activities/service_learning.htm (accessed July 27, 2008).

Vernon, A., and K. Ward. 1999. Campus and community partnerships: Assessing impacts and strengthening connections. *Michigan Journal of Community Service Learning* 6: 30–37.

Vogelgesang, L. J., M. Drummond, and S. K. Gilmartin. 2003. *How higher education is integrating diversity and service learning: Findings from four case studies*. San Francisco: California Campus Compact.

Wade-Golden, K., and J. Matlock. 2007. Ten core ingredients for fostering campus diversity success. *The Diversity Factor* 15 (1): 41–48. www.calvin.edu/admin/provost/multicultural/documents/campusdiversity.pdf (accessed January 22, 2009).

Wallace, J. 2000. The problem of time: Enabling students to make long-term commitments to community-based learning. *Michigan Journal of Community Service Learning* 7: 133–42.

Ward, K., and L. Wolf-Wendel. 2000. Community-centered service learning: Moving from doing for to doing with. *American Behavioral Scientist* 43 (5): 767–80.

Watts-Jones, D. 2002. Healing internalized racism: The role of a within-group sanctuary among people of African Descent. *Family Process* 41 (4): 591–601.

Wayne State College. n.d. *10 Points of project-based service-learning*. http://academic.wsc.edu/service-learning/what_is/10%20Points%20of%20Project_059.pdf (accessed August 6, 2008).

Weah, W., V. C. Simmons, and M. Hall. 2000. Service learning and multicultural/multiethnic perspectives: From diversity to equity. *Phi Delta Kappan* 81 (9): 673–75. www.nylc.org/rc_downloadfile.cfm?emoid=14:250&property=download&mode=download (accessed August 3, 2008).

YWCA Madison. 2008. Online racial justice class. http://rjclass.ywca.org/madison (accessed August 6, 2008).

Contributors

Shannon M. Bell completed her undergraduate education at the University of Wisconsin-Madison with a BA in political science and a minor in African studies. She is currently pursuing a Master of Science in public policy and management from the Heinz College at Carnegie Mellon University with a focus on sustainable development and social entrepreneurship. Her recent projects include social enterprise research at the Institute for Social Innovation, a primary school health and education program in Nicaragua, and research with FINCA International (the Foundation for International Community Assistance) on client-assessment tools.

Rebecca Carlson recently joined on as an ecodesign coordinator for the Tamarisk Coalition, an environmental nonprofit that provides education, technical assistance, and coordinating support for the restoration of riparian lands. Splitting her time between Colorado and Wisconsin, she also gladly volunteers for the Center for Resilient Cities in Madison in between finishing her master's degree in landscape architecture at the University of Wisconsin.

Cassandra Garcia is a PhD student in the Environmental Monitoring Program at the Nelson Institute for Environmental Studies at the University of Wisconsin-Madison. Her research focuses on evaluating the incorporation of Geographic Information Systems (GIS) into public participation processes.

Barbara Golden was a graduate student in educational policy studies at the time of this writing, focusing on the role of African American parents in their children's education. She recently worked as a secondary educator in a public school system, but now devotes her time to her family's business and her role as "nonattorney advocate" for children and families who need—but cannot afford—legal representation.

Jason Gonzalez is a 2010 Juris Doctor candidate at the University of Wisconsin Law School. He received his Bachelor of Science from the University of Wisconsin-Madison in 2007 in legal studies and political science with a certificate in criminal justice. He also completed a senior thesis in legal studies funded by the Audrey J. Harris Legal Studies Research Fellowship. As an undergraduate, he was a Chancellor's/Powers-Knapp Merit Scholar and a Wisconsin Idea Undergraduate Fellow.

Dadit Hidayat is a Nelson Institute of Environmental Studies doctoral student at the University of Wisconsin-Madison. His general interest is in understanding social dynamic within the community in engaging issues of sustainable living. His dissertation's research will focus on sustainable transportation: how community responds to the changing needs of current travel behavior that is not sustainable.

Amy Hilgendorf was an AmeriCorps°VISTA member working with the University of Wisconsin-Extension and Wisconsin Campus Compact at the time of the project. Now a doctoral student at the University of Wisconsin-Madison in human development and family studies, she studies the relations between families and schools and she seeks opportunities to incorporate community-based research into her own research and teaching.

Cynthia Lin is a graduate student at the University of Wisconsin-Madison. Her research seeks to address how grassroots groups can create and sustain autonomous spaces for social change as alternatives to the "nonprofit industrial complex." This work is inspired and informed by the dialogue led by groups like INCITE! Women of Color Against Violence. Cynthia is also involved in local organizing around race and economic justice and would like to acknowledge everyone who has nudged her onto this path.

Amy Martin graduated from the University of Wisconsin-Madison in 2005 with a BA in history and Latin American, Caribbean, and Iberian Studies (LACIS). Upon graduating she volunteered with AmeriCorps VISTA to increase community involvement in the Madison Metropolitan School District. While at VISTA, she contributed to the research for this book through interviewing community groups involved with service learning. She has spent the last few years working with various health-care reform initiatives and plans to attend law school.

Amy S. Mondloch is executive director of the Grassroots Leadership College, a leadership and community organizing training program in Madison, Wisconsin. She has been a community organizer and activist for almost twenty years. Her current community activities include volunteering with WORT 89.9 FM community radio, serving on the board of Clearwater Folk School, being a Big Sister through Big Brothers Big Sisters, and involvement in several labor and political organizations.

Sarah Nehrling is an international education professional and a recent graduate of the University of Wisconsin-Madison. She is editor and translator of the African language primer "Gan Gi: An Introduction to Modern Wolof," and recently completed an International Foundation for Education and Self-Help (IFESH) Literacy Fellowship in Cote d'Ivoire. She is currently serving as volunteer program coordinator for Tostan International, a community development nongovernmental organization (NGO) based in Senegal, West Africa.

Samuel Pratsch is a PhD dissertator in the Gaylord Nelson Institute for Environmental Studies at the University of Wisconsin-Madison. His dissertation is focused on understanding the root causes of land-use change in the *paramo* (a high Andean ecosystem) of Venezuela. His overall goal is to encourage farmers to become stewards of the *paramo* and to support the design and implementation of alternative land-use strategies that conserve *paramo*, while meeting the needs of farmers living and working there. Samuel aspires to become a professor of environmental studies and continue to use participatory research methods in his future studies.

Charity Schmidt was in the Latin American, Caribbean, and Iberian Studies Master's Program at the University of Wisconsin-Madison at the time of this writing, and she now studies there as a PhD student in rural sociology. She worked for several years with Randy Stoecker on the statewide project to improve the community impact of service learning in Wisconsin. Her current research is on urban land reform and grassroots movements in Venezuela. She is active with several community groups that focus on Latin American politics as well as relations between Latin America and the United States.

Ian Scott is a community and urban planner working for the town of View Royal in British Columbia, Canada. He graduated with a master's in urban and regional planning from the University of Wisconsin-Madison, where he focused his studies and research on the means people have to make positive change in their community—as advocates, through community service, and as extension researchers, urban designers, and planners.

Kristy SeBlonka graduated in 2007 from the Department of Urban and Regional Planning, University of Wisconsin, with a concentration in community and economic development. She is currently volunteering in Nicaragua. Upon return to the United States, she plans to continue working for just and democratic community development.

Randy Stoecker is professor in the Department of Community and Environmental Sociology at the University of Wisconsin-Madison with a joint appointment at the University of Wisconsin-Extension Center for Community and Economic Development. He is the moderator and editor of COMM-ORG: The On-Line Conference on Community Organizing and Development at http://comm-org.wisc.edu, the author of *Research Methods for Community Change*, and a coauthor of *Community-Based Research and Higher Education*. He is currently working on a statewide project to improve the community impact of service learning and grassroots civic engagement in Wisconsin.

Elizabeth Tryon is community partner specialist for the Human Issues Studies Program at Edgewood College, Madison, Wisconsin. She coordinates service learning for students, collaborates with community agencies on partnership activities and advocacy work, and presents her research on community perceptions of service learning at conferences in the United States, Canada, and Europe. She has published several journal articles on service learning and community engagement, and coauthored a book chapter on information and communication technology in service learning.

Index

The idea differs significantly from community service models seen in traditional service learning placements in that everyone involved in the process, including faculty, staff, committee members, program participants, and volunteers, are all seen as contributors to the process who have a great deal to share as well as to learn, and who have a responsibility to direct the organization. The organization is dynamic and able to flex to the needs determined by the community rather than committed to a static system of programs that provide services.

In the case of the Grassroots Leadership College, this has meant significant modifications in our core programs each semester. These modifications come from the feedback of participants through evaluations, focus groups, and continuing discussions, as well as the observations of staff, committee, and board members, and the interests of volunteer faculty. It also has meant the addition of a place-based series on Madison's South Side and a series of organizing workshops offered in Spanish, as well. Both of these programs developed through the interests of community members, alumni, board members, and allied organizations.

The service learner becomes an integral part of the decision-making process. This begins on the first day, when the learner meets with staff to determine what the person wants to learn as well as what expertise he or she can share. Through this process, the learning project is sculpted. It is a considerably more complicated process than more traditional organizations in which a learner is simply given tasks, but we believe it fosters ownership and encourages long-term community involvement.

Creating the Space for Leadership by Service Learners

Starting from the motto above, the GLC begins every service learning relationship with the understanding that we will teach the learner some skills. We will share some ideas and experiences. We'll also have some opportunities to open ourselves to learning new skills and to grow from the ideas and experiences of the learner. When we remember this, great things happen. When we forget, we all lose.

This is a new experience for many service learners who have been indoctrinated by the formal educational system for much of their lives. Unfortunately, many traditional college students have had few experiences with self-determination. That means we sometimes need to practice a bit of patience and hold their hand in the beginning until they develop a sense of trust in the staff with whom they work, allowing them to contribute more creative ideas and carry out those thoughts. That hand-holding comes in the form of asking lots of questions, expressing appreciation for their work, and gently encouraging them to keep thinking deeply and strategically.

Doing the Groundwork

As nonprofit leaders, we look around ourselves and see communities with many needs. We stretch meager budgets and limited staffing to serve a broad array of clients or constituents. We often are drawn to see service learners in one of two lights: (1) "Look, a new volunteer who can give us time, great! We need another worker bee!" or (2) "Ugh, another volunteer to supervise. I don't think I can do one more thing!" While both responses make a lot of sense in the stress-filled world of nonprofits, neither is particularly useful for the long-term success of our work. Looking to our future is particularly important today, as the baby boomers that led the way for expansion of social services and grassroots groups in the 1960s and 1970s are now looking to retirement, and we who are left need to figure out creative ways to fill the gaps left by those who led our field for more than thirty years.

There are a few questions to guide the process of laying the groundwork for a successful, forward-looking service learning experience:

- How does service learning fit within our mission and vision?
- How will this relationship and project move our work forward?
- What resources do we have to give to this relationship?
- What resources do we have to maintain and build the work beyond this learner's term with the organization? Is it sustainable?
- What are our expectations for the experience? Are those expectations shared by the faculty and the learner?

You'll notice that the service learner is hardly mentioned until near the end in the list of questions. That is intentional; we need to do a lot of thoughtful work before opening the door.

Fitting the Mission and Vision

It all begins with that little phrase that lights your organizational fire. For the GLC, it's two things: the vision, "Everyone a Learner, Everyone a Teacher, Everyone a Leader," and the mission, "to support the development of grassroots leaders by building skills and relationships in a supportive and challenging environment." Whether you are saving manatees or making sure every child learns to read, the service learning program needs to feed the fire of that mission and vision or it will be a cold and dark night.

In a climate where resources such as funding, staffing, volunteers, and other necessities are perceived as scarce, it is easy to reach out for what is available in the moment to fill a gap without a full understanding of the impact of our actions. For the GLC, the problem of scarcity looks like this: Every few weeks someone comes to us with a great idea of a workshop we should do, a population we should work with, something we should do. Generally, the ideas are great! We should start a teen program. We should expand our reach further into the various Asian communities. We should hold weekend institutes. Sure, we would love to do all those things and some company, grant maker, or donor might love to fund them. But what would that mean for our staff, for our volunteers? How would it affect how we see ourselves, our mission, and our vision? Could we sustain all the work we do? It's time for a deep breath. It's time to sit with all the options and figure out what makes sense for us right now, what would make sense in the future, and what we can let someone else carry out.

We've learned that perceived scarcity coupled by the changing interests of foundations on which many of our groups depend, often leads to expansion or change of direction in programming. Too often the question becomes "Could we get funding for this project?" instead of "How does this project meet our interests as an organization?"

Thus begins the downward spiral of growing just to survive, allowing our mission to drift in hopes of being able to keep our doors open. Such mission drift, which starts in an effort to expand our capabilities and do greater good, often actually makes resources increasingly scarce. It causes clients, constituents, volunteers, and staff to lose connectedness to a shared purpose defined by the organizational mission and vision statements. We begin to wander, lost, as the organizational fire dies away, leaving us without the light and heat that drive us.

Service learning can be fuel for the fire or it can be more sticks thrown helter-skelter into the woods. It's up to us to be conscious of where we put our efforts and to what ends. It all depends on how that learner's experience reflects the mission and vision.

In the Grassroots Leadership College, one role that volunteers and sometimes service learners fill is that of coach. Each coach in the program works with one or two developing leaders over about four months. Together they attend a series of classes that cover basic community organizing skills such as seeing self as leader, fund-raising, conflict transformation, conducting effective meetings, and others. These sessions are taught by volunteer faculty who work either professionally or in a volunteer capacity on the particular skill set that they teach. The education process is based in small and large group activities, reflection, and conversation directed by the needs of the participants. While participants are sometimes directed to supplementary readings if they want additional resources, classes are not reading dependent. Exams are not a part of the process. Education is led by the participants through an initial needs-and-wants assessment, a continued evaluation process, and an interactive classroom model that respects the idea that everyone in the room learns, teaches, and leads.

Coach and developing leader teams also meet at least four times outside of the classroom to strategize on a project designed by the developing leader. The coach is not a mentor; he or she is not expected to be the expert on the project area. Coaches are expected to provide a listening ear and to ask lots of questions that help the developing leader create a strategy to address his or her project. Coaches may also share resources and direct the developing leader to possible project supporters or directly provide assistance to the effort, keeping in mind that the developing leader is the person in charge of directing the work and the coach is simply a support.

That experience can be a great way of looking at how an individual volunteer or service learner fits the vision "Everyone a learner, everyone a teacher, everyone a leader" and how that fit helps determine the long-term outcome.

Coach One, let's call her Tamika, takes that vision statement pretty seriously. When she meets with her developing leader, Sue, who is or-